AT ALBERTA

NATHALIE STEPHENS

BookThug | Toronto
MMVIII

TABLE OF CONTENTS

WANT : L'INTRADUISIBLE
(DESIRE IN TRANSLATION)   7

ALÉA   OF WHICH WE ARE A PART
         OF WHICH WE ARE ... APART   18

CORRESPONDANCES
MONTRÉAL ... CHICAGO ... WHEREVER   38

FROM ASTRAY TO ESTRANGED
(SELF-)TRANSLATING CLAUDE CAHUN   44

AFTER ALBERTA (I)
STILL (T)HERE BY ANNE MALENA   54

AFTER ALBERTA (II)
WHAT ARCHITECTURES OF URGENCY
DO YOU RAISE? AND THEN RAZE?
WITH CHRISTINE STEWART   63

FIRST EDITION

copyright © Nathalie Stephens, 2008
"Still (T)here" copyright © Anne Malena, 2008
additional text copyright © Christine Stewart, 2008

Produced with the generous assisstance of the
Canada Council for the Arts and the Ontario Arts
Council.

 Canada Council   Conseil des Arts
for the Arts   du Canada

 ONTARIO ARTS COUNCIL
CONSEIL DES ARTS DE L'ONTARIO

LIBRARY AND ARCHIVES CANADA
CATALOGUING IN PUBLICATION

Stephens, Nathalie, 1970-
At Alberta / Nathalie Stephens.

(Department of critical thought ; 1)
Includes some text in French.
ISBN 978-1-897388-24-0

I. Title. II. Series.

PS8587.T375A88 2008   C814'.54   C2008-904548-3

PRINTED IN CANADA

WANT : L'INTRADUISIBLE
(DESIRE IN TRANSLATION)

I WILL BEGIN WITH THE 'failure of translation'. If one can speak at all of beginnings. Before even approaching the 'failure of language.' I have arrived, we have all arrived here – *here* – mid-conversation, as it were. As if it were … possible to pick up where others have left off, without being subsumed into what Catherine Clément describes so exhaustively as syncope, a moment of absence, of retreat, disappearance, removal, to a here, not here, there somewhere, unaccountable, but for which we are, must be, accountable, somehow, somewhere.

Here, then. What I call here shall be 'the failure of translation'. A place, liminal, interstitial, abyssal – all of these – into which we fall, as one might fall in love, breakingly, or else fall apart, devastatingly, catching on the pieces of our own ruination, jaggedly, tearingly, seemingly (seamingly?). Fall away, imperceptibly. Still, the leurre of falling, is that the movement finds completion. It is not so at all; I have not found it to be so. Is it possible, here, in this moment of failure, of 'the failure of translation' (begun before even beginning), to evoke a fall without drawing into this space, a whole exegetical mess? I do hope so. I would like to find fall (find fault?) in a bodily way, with all the bruising this entails, the marking of the body, and the inscription of the fall in the body's tissue. A downward movement that stops at the breath, that stops at nothing, carried into and by the breath, such that it, the fall, becomes indistinguishable from our own exhalation. We may find, in the end, which is of course neverending, that our failure, the place into which we fall, is the very thing that catches us. But we aren't quite there yet.

In *Writing and Madness,* Shoshana Felman writes (in collaborative translation) : "If the 'failure of translation' between languages is in some sense radically irreducible, what is at stake in the passage from one language to another is less translation in itself than the translation of oneself – into the otherness of languages. To speak about madness is to speak about the difference between languages: to import into one language the strangeness of another; to unsettle the decisions language has prescribed to us so that, somewhere between languages, will emerge the freedom to speak."[1]

It might be relevant, here, to cite the same passage from *La folie et la chose littéraire,*

Felman again, en français: "Or, si le 'défaut de traduction' est entre les langues, quelque part, radicalement irréductible, il s'agit, en passant d'une langue à une autre, en franchissant la limite entre langues, non pas tant (et non pas simplement) de traduire, que de se traduire à l'altérité des langues. Parler de la folie, c'est parler de la différence entre langues : faire passer à travers une langue l'étrangeté d'une autre; chercher à ébranler, dans chaque langue, les décisions linguistiques qu'elle prescrit à notre parole, afin qu'émerge entre les langues, dans un lieu indécidable, la liberté de parler."[2]

I will speak of madness. Speak of madness from a reserve of desire. Speak of impotence in this place underwritten by jouissance. We can't all be hard all of the time, and desire, in this instance, may well be located, furtively, within the interstitial 'failure' of translation. The faille, the fault line, the rupture that is given form when

with our bodies we disrupt the limits,
not just of language, of languages, but of
ourselves.

A curious fracture occurs in this passage —
in at least two senses of passage, the
textual and the transitional, and in all
the senses granted to sense. Passage: the
passage into the otherness of language.
Moving backwards from failure of
translation to le défaut de la traduction.
The equivalence is wonderfully
instructive: failure for défaut. Failure,
which might otherwise translate into
French as échec, or faille, or manquement.
Défaut, as defect, flaw, fault, shortcoming,
and yes, failing, as it pertains to people.
Failure is something one arrives at. With
défaut, one is already there. And here we
are now inside this 'failure' which I have
offered as a substitution for place, as place
itself, this place, which I have suggested
be designated by here, a here that is of
course unreachable because it is the place

where we are and the place we have yet to arrive at.

There is the suggestion, in Felman's phraseology, in this apprehension of passage, of the foundational. "Irreducible," she writes. I would like to leave this foundationality alone for a moment and turn instead, to the dislocations – the syncopes perhaps – that occur concomittantly, to the body that moves into the otherness of language and to the languages into and from which it moves. How this encounter is by its very undertaking, fractured, and how this fracture, a violent, incontrovertible and desirable consequence of dislocation, of displacement, is determining for the expression of desire, of desire's inexpressibility, in and outside of ('the failure of') translation. And how, as a result, desire, in translation, its reserve, is an expression scattered with the ashes of grief, suffused, abysally, with the

unboundedness of mourning, drenched
with that same madness, with that
inexpressibility, caught in that aporia of
feeling.

In translation, I stand at a threshold. The
translation itself stands at a threshold.
Its, my, our, position is liminal, always.
Translation, from the Latin, *translatus*,
for 'carried across'. What we carry must
be lifted and borne. What we carry risks
further disintegration in the course of its
passage. (Further because, before even we
arrive at the threshold of the text, on a
verge of translation, the process of decay is
already begun. It precedes us and exceeds
us). None of it remains intact. Not the
text from which we borrow, not that
which we maim. Nor the body, our own,
and the many others, that fall to pieces as
we come into contact with them.
*Translation (fr): le fait de transporter
(les restes, le corps d'une personne);* the
transportation (of remains, of the body of

a person). This body which is no longer body, but impossibly suffused with love nonetheless, that comes apart in our hands, and leaves imperceptible stains at the points at which we touch. Body for bruise. We trade in dust.

To translate is to touch. And as I have indicated elsewhere, while it may very well be impossible to establish an ethics of translation outside of the act of questioning itself, we may approach an ethics of touch through the acknowledgement of the bodies with which we come into contact, and their fragility, ours as well. Even though and perhaps because what we touch we touch unwittingly. We may envisage an ethics of touch that is relational, that is one of encounter, that anticipates our own otherness in the other whom (or which) we approach, approaches us, with all of the bodily after-effects, the exchange of breath, of fluids, of affect and affectation, of affection and tumult, violation.

"Between you and it there is a reciprocity of giving: you say You to it and give yourself to it; it says You to you and gives itself to you. You cannot come to an understanding about it with others; you are lonely with it; but it teaches you to encounter others and to stand your ground in such encounters; and through the grace of its advents and the melancholy of its departures it leads you to that You in which the lines of relation, though parallel, intersect. It does not help you to survive; it only helps you to have intimations of eternity."[3]

We, body and text, are porous – disarmingly, disastrously, maddenningly, seductively, murderously permeable. Buber's 'reciprocity of giving' implies a 'reciprocity of taking'. And it is here that we lose ourselves, risk losing ourselves. Because, away from what onanistic excitements might hover at the surface of this practice, conceivable as many different forms of seduction and fucking, of penetration and orgasm, within a phallocentric economy of translation which does not preclude every form of violation, are questions that undermine the safe veneer of performativity in which our time finds such dissociated comfort – that implicate the whole of the fractured, displaced, self. I am not suggesting here that translation as a practice of eroticism is not possible, nor even desirable, but that the consequences of such a gesture are necessarily embedded in the historical moment in which we articulate want, and in which desire, not limited to the realm of carnality, is cast from a vast expanse of sadness. Buber's reciprocity of giving, two letters short of a reciprocity of grieving, envisions encounter as loss. In the apprehension of vastness, we are no closer to surviving ("it does not help you to survive"); simply, we come into

contact with, we touch the thing that
eludes us. We touch beside touching.
We grieve beside grief. We mourn what
is insurmountable. We desire with the
knowledge that what we desire is lost to
us, is loss itself.

"The intersection of the lines of relation"
brings the body to one threshold that
touches another. In crossing these lines,
we transport ourselves into the space
of the other. However artificial these
boundaries – whose forms are most
dramatically, most violently evident at
the border crossings between countries
(witness, for example, the consequences
of Walter Benjamin's attempt at passage
into Spain in 1940; or the intransigeantly
guarded gates into and out of Israel) – a
translation occurs as the body moves over
the line, carrying itself as a remnant to be
reconstituted on the other, aleatory, side;
the passage threatens always to dissolve
what passes, in the form of time, of space,

of body, each in contact with the other, and at times several bodies at once, in just as many directions.

Felman makes a distinction between 'translation in itself' and the 'translation of oneself'. There is an ethical imperative to the latter construction that is, or may be, absent from the former. 'Translation in itself' maintains a safe distance (but from what?), positions translation, as an activity undertaken away from the body, away from the translator, and this despite the many formulations of (in)fidelity that have many times been debated. The question of fidelity arguably removes translation from the public (political) sphere and ensconces the act safely in the boudoir where pages turn in domestic privacy, for one's own pain and delectation. We kiss the text in quiet.

At times – often – it devours us. The 'translation of oneself' makes clear this risk, positioning the body squarely where it already is, which is to say, spacially, temporally, between. It stands, unrealised, in anticipation of itself, and in cognisant fear of its imminent dispersal.

The desire to translate, to translate oneself, is a desire to come into being in another form, through a language that might be able to hold what eludes the translator, of text, of self (this, at any rate, is the ideal). But the wager is such that this gesture of encounter, whether with myself or with another, is predicated upon its dispersal – regardless of intent. In reaching for another possible utterance, a further articulation of itself, it not only anticipates its own death, but invites it. Desire, in translation, is wrought of loss, and what it hopes to restore, it consigns, unwittingly, to oblivion. The passage delineated by the trace, the transcription, a palimpsestic device, becomes one of devastation. In the passage of oneself from one language into another, in the expression of a desire for further and more, the space that opens, that offers itself as here, the failure, the faille, is poised between murder and suicide; there is no natural death to speak of. I translate myself. We translate ourselves. That is, we carry ourselves, the part of us that remains at the moment of crossing, into the space of the other. This transfer, by its etymology and its reluctant generosity – 'what gives takes' might be a reformulation of Buber's text – engages our willingness to leave something (of ourselves) behind. It places trust in the other; it vindicates the line; and with each crossing, back and forth, with each pause somewhere, there, at the place between, we carry out gestures of mourning, we complete the action of giving with grieving. We acknowledge, in this instant, and in this place, our failure to make encounter complete. It is this fracture, this fragmentation, of

ourselves, of translation, and of the text
in our bruised and bruising hands, which
undermines the expression of a desire
(traditionally expressed romantically as
a desire for completion or wholeness)
indistinguishable from the loss from
which it arises.

The 'failure of translation' is also the
'failure of language', and it is here that
desire finds furtive, fractured form.
Formidably. Forbiddingly. In *La carte
postale*, Derrida writes : "Tu as raison,
nous sommes sans doute plusieurs et je
ne suis pas si seul que je le dis parfois
quand la plainte m'en est arrachée ou que
je m'évertue encore à te séduire."[4] The
name, in this case, Jacques Derrida's,
in the form of a signature, a seduction,
is multiplied and rent. And what
accompanies this expression of desire,
unlanguaged, isolated (in his claim to a
feeling of aloneness) is a cry, that has no
form other than the sound from which

and into which it emerges, shattered, torn. It is through striving, through the attempt to make passage, to(ward) the other (the lover) that the cry supplants the articulation of desire which is not ever realised. Two movements occur concomittantly: striving and wrenching. One, striving, is a manifestation of the will; the other, wrenching, is exerted from outside, subjugating and imposed. It is perhaps not possible to envision one without the other, desire without enclosure, freedom without constraint, language without the cry. And not silence, as one might anticipate. Not silence, because silence is in language; the cry is possibly a gesture (impossible) away from language, from the strictures that bind the body to a form of expression of its own design and which proves itself, again and again, to be inadequate. Because of our presence in it? What we touch falls to ruin. There is ample evidence of this all around, in our trampled cities, in the

fields we do and do not cultivate, in the
disappearance of our oceans, in the wars
that abound, in the voice that falters,
over and again. And so it stands to reason
that translation – and as such touch – is,
if not equatable with failure, a harbinger
of failure (of falling), of destruction,
one of its possible manifestations. In the
reach away, we find ourselves caught.
Which brings me to one of Buber's most
powerful formulations, locating the
bind in the torment of freedom itself:
"And to gain freedom from the belief in
unfreedom is to gain freedom."[5]

We are not so far from where we began,
the place reaching toward what Felman
calls the "freedom to speak." "Somewhere
between languages," she writes " will
emerge the freedom to speak." Even
between languages, one is speaking in
relation to language, in the "reciprocity of
giving", of grieving. Leaving one another
behind.

How is it that location becomes so determining in this conversation? That the 'failure of translation' takes on the characteristics of place, of a bordered here or a there, to be arrived at or left, inhabited, traversed, remembered, relocated, or necessarily, impossibly, restored. In other words not just temporally but spacially determined as well. *In absentia*, always, since we are always just outside of its reach or it ours, missing one another at the moment of exchange, into which we fall, blunderingly, deliberately, and bereft of ability, we are surrendered to the caprice of language's deceit and our willing participation in it.

Another curious *glissement* or slippage occurs in the penultimate clause of the Felman passage on passage. What is carried into English as "somewhere between languages", is inscribed, in

French as "dans un lieu indécidable".
In an undecidable place. Between as it
occurs, and eludes me in my own work,
entre-genre and entre-langues – between
genders, genres, between languages – is
a fluid, fluctuant, indeterminate place, a
place in movement, always, and as such
unlocatable, but relational. Indécidable
expresses a desire for foundation, a reach
toward a kind of stability that is not
available to us in language as elsewhere.
Indécidable, a mathematical term, cannot
be sumitted either to refutation nor to
proofs. It goes further than between into
absence. Indécidable is what cannot be
touched nor inhabited, what eludes the
rational, Cartesian, trappings that would
fix it, once and for all. Felman locates
madness somewhere else, "somewhere at
that point of silence where it is no longer
we who speak, but where, in our absence,
we are spoken." L'indécidable might be
that absent space into which we fall, into
which we disappear, in the abyss opened

by the 'failure of translation' which is none other than loss, the only possible place from which we might begin to articulate, inarticulably, the desire that underwrites, in a language of its own, unavailable to us, the ways in which we touch, might touch.

However ironically, these dislocations, these strange temperaments and temptations, actually enable encounter; they enable the expression of desire, which traverses the body into the text, through innumerable interchangeable intersecting circuits that entangle one with other, such that in touching through text to the other, we touch, not just ourselves – onanistically, sometimes self-destructively – but the untouched untouchable part that awaits, seductively, undecidably. Untouchable, not because it is unrivalled or unbreakable, but because it remains out of our grasp. Undecidable, for the part of us that is not yet incarcerated in

the systems of language, the systems of
thought which bait us with constraint. So
we are left reaching, and the ethics of our
endeavour lies there. Poised, on a verge,
replete with desire, and depleting.

In the turn toward the body – the
distances installed between body and
language – is an impossible gesture
of retrieval. It is the admission, the
admonition, the avowal of the body's own
muted dislocation.

The reserve of desire might be in a name,
withheld : the one spoken, and the one
swallowed, neither of which is consumed,
neither of which is consummated.
Because to say body is already to fix in
language a manner for desire, a manner
for touch, a manner for movement which
is seized in a lingual space of compromise
and capitulation. "Tu rêves pour pouvoir
dire son nom, mais dès que tu le dis, le
nom explose dans ta gorge, les débris

t'étouffent et tu te réveilles pour vomir."⁶

The name may not only be unspeakable but undesirable, even as it holds that reserve of desire, in a soundless, other place. It may, in this case, be what the body rejects, in the form, here, of vomit and remains. It is what remains of us. It is what makes of us : remains. And in the body's emergence from itself, the spill of what is otherwise contained, in the viscous pore (pour) of language, languages, we translate. We re-form… ulate the body's own plural text; we submit it to (its) disintegration, we want the thing that is unavailable to us, the thing that language does not hold; the part that is body, in and outside of text that multiplies, enfolds.

There is insufficient time to expose all of my terms, to contextualise their relationship to one another and the (mis) uses I have made of them. If what I have described is akin to wreckage and ill-disposed to salvage, it is no less imperative that it find formulation, even failed formulation, with the recognition of its failure. It is no less urgent to reach toward an expression of touch in translation, to locate touch inside translation, its failure, our faults. History demands it, but so do the ethics that govern our work and our responsibility to the present.

I would like to conclude with a brief return to Derrida, and desire. In a 1999 interview entitled "Le siècle et le pardon", Derrida offers this among his cautions: "il n'y a de pardon, s'il y en a, que de l'impardonnable."[7] He is responding, in the wake of the Shoah, to Vladimir Jankélévitch's polemical refusal, after Auschwitz, to forgive. "Le pardon," provokes Jankélevitch, "est mort dans les camps de la mort."[8] To which Derrida, through very meticulous argumentation, formalised in *Pardonner: l'impardonnable et l'imprescriptible*[9], arrives at this ethical aporia : that the only possible forgiveness consists in forgiving the unforgiveable; a point he further developed in other work. I do not wish to open a conversation on the unforgiveable necessarily, nor to make a simple graft of translatability onto Derrida's formulation. I do, nonetheless, wish to draw out the implications of (un)translatability and to suggest that they bear a comparable ethical weight with the unresolvable question of the pardon. To point to a poignant and likely problematic relationship between the unforgiveable and the untranslatable. Again and again, we say that despite the failure of translation, we must translate, that despite the many obstacles to and within translation, we must continue to cross these borders, whatever the risk, to the body of the text, to our own bodies. This must is governed by an ethical imperative that reaches toward the body of language. "C'est-à-dire que la vie de

la langue," Derrida insists "c'est aussi
le travail du deuil; c'est aussi le deuil
impossible."[10] I cannot help but ask now:
Where does translation die? I offer this in
reply: it dies inside of us. We anticipate
its death, we facilitate it, and through our
work, the impossible work of mourning,
we touch what is already gone. We carry
it. Whatever desire we encounter, in us, in
the text, between the various intervening
bodies, is imbued with this impossible
work of mourning. It determines our
ability to reach. And what we reach
toward is not death itself, but its echo. In
the unforgivable, as in the untranslatable,
there is an absence to contend with. Our
own anticipated absence, and the absence
of the other.

Untranslatability is precisely translation's
aporia. Our translational struggle (at
the edge of what river? by whose hand
bruised? and in what name?) locates itself,
failingly, within untranslatability – within

the untouchable, unspeakable reserve of
desire coiled in the belly of our texts, in
the place where, imperfectly, they come to
touch one another; the lines that we cross,
the gulf that swallows us. And it is here,
in this gulf, this abyss, here, which I called
to begin with 'the failure of translation',
from here this failure that desire emerges,
only here that desire can emerge, if at all.

Loss in desire. Desire from loss. Desire
because of loss.

Suffused with the sorrow, our outpouring
and our arrestation, that saturates our
work, when we touch the thing into
which we fall, when we attempt to carry
what we fail, what falls into us, through
us, and away. What, of its remains, we
betray. Desire is the expression of loss's
desire to salvage itself. And it is in that
place that we move. We begin inside loss
and we remain there. We begin inside the
body and we remain there. There : "on

reçoit un corps et on y laisse sa signature."
There : inside loss, which enables us, not
to desire what is lost, but to desire loss.
To feel loss in desire. Without which, we
are unable to touch, with our bodies, the
cry that persists in our mouths, that resists
language's bind, freeing itself into the
undecidable place where desire anticipates
our translated remains.

            Chicago, August 2006

1. Translated by Martha Noel Evans and the author with Brian Massumi, Ithaca (NY), Cornell University Press, 1985, p. 19.
2. Paris, Éditions du Seuil, p. 18-19.
3. Martin Buber, *I and Thou*, trans. Walter Kaufmann, New York, Simon and Schuster, 1970, p. 84
4. Jacques Derrida, *La Carte Postale*, Paris, Flammarion, 1980, p. 10. ("You are right, we are several no doubt and I am not as alone as I sometimes claim to be when the cry is wrenched from me or I still strive to seduce you.")
5. *I and Thou*, p. 107.
6. Hélène Cixous, *Préparatifs de noces au-delà de l'abîme*, Paris, des femmes, 1978, p. 16. ("You dream of being able to say the name, but as soon as you do, the name explodes in your throat, the debris suffocates you and you awaken to vomit.")
7. Jacques Derrida, "Le siècle et le pardon," entretien, *Le monde des débats*, décembre 1999.
8. Jankélévitch cited by Jacques Derrida in *Pardonner*, p. 28 ("Forgiveness died in the death camps.")
9. Paris, Cahiers de L'Herne, 2005.
10. Jacques Derrida, "La langue n'appartient pas," entretien réalisé avec Évelynne Grossman, *Europe, Paul Celan*, no. 861-862, January-February, 2001, p. 88 ("The life of language […] is also the work of mourning; it is also impossible mourning." Trans. Thomas Dutoit and Philippe Romanski, *Sovereignties in Question: The Poetics of Paul Celan*, p. 103).

ALÉA OF WHICH WE ARE A PART
OF WHICH WE ARE ... APART

Now where is my where?
> – Mahmoud Darwich

*Maintenant je suis maudit, j'ai horreur
de la patrie.*
> – Arthur Rimbaud

*For the space of the prospect and its clarity
seemed to offer no impediment whatsoever,
but to allow our lives to spread out and out
beyond all bristling of roofs and chimneys to
the flawless verge.*
> – Virginia Woolf

BERLIN, JE M'EN DOUTAIS, *mais moi aussi j'aime ne pas savoir. Que la ville soit nulle part et ailleurs tout à la fois. » C'est donc de Berlin qu'il s'agit lorsque B. m'écrit « this city ». En juillet comme d'ailleurs à tous les autres moments de l'année, « this city » ne se matérialise que dans l'espace éployé entre deux lettres. Cet espace est aussi vaste et insondable que les fonds des océans, et aussi étroit qu'une rigole. « This city » n'est, bien entendu, ni Berlin, ni Lisbonne, et localisable sur aucune carte géographique, mais prend forme entre deux corps qui s'écrivent sur la distance inimitable d'une amitié. Ces ouvertures – ces ébrasures – sont* *le propre de l'*incriture; *l'intimité ouverte sur un monde pris au dépourvu.*[1]

City: undecided, misunderstood or non-existent, the body situates itself provisionally in relation to it, presses against its sparse intimacy capable of beginning and reducing, if not exhausting, a correspondence. By correspondence, I mean not only those letters we send one another, that are written, sealed, opened, read and burned, but the space somewhat spent by the effort deployed to immerse oneself – raw touch, say, which (b)reaches the body in the non-sense of sensuality, in its proximity to the ground, where everything slips away – *dérape* – : elsewhere.[2]

In this (incensed) sense, *le dérapage* (slippage) is far from being a point of arrival, as much as it is a turn capable of upsetting or undoing a conjured movement. Such a moment displays the artifice of cities, for having been made, but also for having been occupied, in other words: said. Let's leave aside any teleological or determining preoccupation, which is of no interest in a space whose Cartesian design is evidence especially of the (f)rigidity of its designers (a Le Corbusier, say, or a Mies van der Rohe) and poorly conceals a vibrant aleatory, present in a city's circuits (a disoriented Gaudí comes to mind, sleeping on his work site, planting mushrooms in rock and undulating limestone). *Le dérapage* makes of ground, not the foundation usually assigned to it, but a symbolic space of the unexpected, undoing a city from its boundaries, a door from its hinge, a passage from its passersby. It opens what appears to be closed, and dematerialises what wishes to be firm, formed, formulated.

While thinking in this way last year, I found myself approaching an elaboration of an ethics of correspondence which offered itself precisely against what manifests itself – without ever naming itself thus – through the parcelling or partitioning of the vast affective (often infected) terrain of literature, or of the textual, which, in spite of itself, remains so fiercely delineated.[3] The *Carnet de désaccords*, still under construction, lifted surreptitiously from *…s'arrête? Je,* and wishing itself to be a manifestation of the "livre erreur"[4] , might be a simultaneous manifestation of errance and interval, indecision and smear. Certainly, it does not say what it is and renounces its own limits, the limits of genre, while taking (necessary) distance from them.

What more instructive space than the city through which to think writing? If only in part because the parcelling, or the partitioning, which divides texts into genres, and bookstores into unfortunate aisles, gridding in this way a highly

governed practice that smugly polices
itself, partakes of a fiercely territorial
tendency, and appears to want to seal
itself to the maddened historical moment
we are presently experiencing in the West,
by granting itself an ironclad, suffocating
identity. The literature of my day has a
stale air about it.

My resistance, then, to the ease (or the
lack of imagination) of delineation – of
genre, and, not incidentally, of gender
(which occupy the same semantic space
in French) –, is tied to a rigorous and
engaged practice of indecision, putting
me in a somewhat compromised position
in relation to my contemporaries; I am
nonetheless disinclined to conform to
expectation as I continue stubbornly to
distance myself from current capitulative
trends. I think I can explain myself; not
by choosing one camp over another[5], but
by throwing into question the practice of
territorialisation itself, as well as its effects,

which st(r)ain the very language I am
using to call attention to them.

§

*Nous n'apprenons rien des bâtiments en nous
limitant à une étude de leurs façades – leurs
portes, leurs fenêtres et leurs murs. Leurs
encadrements (bois, métal, vinyl) et leur
revêtement (stucs, alu, maçonnerie de pierre,
de briques, de plâtre). Ouvertures et parures.
Transparence et subterfuge. Fermeture
et frime. Depuis mon premier voyage à
Chicago, les bâtiments se sont présentés sous
une forme nouvelle, ils m'ont offert un autre
sens, une façon inattendue de les aborder.
Par la toiture. Il y a là matière à réflexion.
Ayant vécu dans des villes qui privilégient
les transports en commun souterrains, je ne
m'attendais pas à ce que soit chamboulé mon
aperçu d'une ville par le simple fait d'un
rail élevé qui suit son chemin centenaire
à la même hauteur que, parfois même
surplombant, les édifices d'une grande partie*

des quartiers résidentiels. Ainsi se voit exposé l'aspect le plus intime d'un bâtiment : sa couverture.[6]

In her essay devoted to the colonial organisation of the city of Algiers – al-Djazair –, Zeynep Çelik notes that "…the houses of the Casbah closed themselves to the street and turned onto a courtyard surrounded by elaborate arcades. The geographic and topographic conditions of Algiers added another element to the houses of the Casbah : rooftop terraces. In contrast to the interiorised courtyards and relatively contrived rooms of the houses, the terraces opened up to neighbors, to the city, to the sea – to the world. The concern for privacy, so dominant in defining the street facades, disintegrated at roof level."[7] If, in this essay, Çelik grants her attention to the separation of the sexes as reflected in the division between public and private spaces, overwritten by the colonialist interpretation (appropriation) that were made of these, she leaves in her language, in her way of speaking rooftops, traces that I uncover with the attention of an archeologist; the same consideration she employed leaving them there. For these terraced rooftops are the privileged space of possibility.

In this passage, two subordinate terms claim my attention : by this I mean that in appearances they serve Çelik's thought ornamentally, but in my view, in the substrata of her essay, they take a (philosophical) place that is not in the least bit accessory. There is on the one hand, the notion of *disintegration* ("The concern for privacy … disintegrated"), and on the other, of *opening* ("… the terraces opened … to the world."). Each requires leaning against a thing other than oneself, a lean against and sometimes immersion into possibility (the world) which is also the unexpected (disintegration), in order to touch, if

only in the abstract, the potentiality of
elsewhere. What offers itself as (or claims
for itself) a cultural space of intimacy, is
the same space given over to reach, to an
other place. According to Le Corbusier,
every house in Algiers had a view of the
sea : "car de chaque logis, de la terrasse
– et ces terrasses additionnées font
comme un magique escalier gigantesque
descendant à la mer – on voit l'espace,
la mer."[8] The proximity of these upward
moments of building to the open invite
the rethinking of territorialisation, and
the notion of conquest, of possession,
implicit in the epistemological act of
nomination, for "the knowledge of things
resides in name".[9]

Through this formulation, rooftops
have the capacity to be the generous
(generative) and singular space of
unlimited potentiality: writing. Their
paradoxical intimacy (paradoxical
precisely because they are open to the

world), their vulnerability (to inclement weather), and their isolation (from the ground), make of them a space both discrete and revealing, toward an imagined, volatile, slippery ground, from which to constitute an ontology of unbound, unanchored letters, drenched in mournful waters while propelling themselves toward an unseizable sky.[10] Neither in flight, nor moored, nor floating, the rooftop carries in an aporetic gesture the paradox of interiority encased in the implicit distances of liminality. A threshold without being one – and carrier of the real danger of thresholds, but also the force of multiple trajectories : "The threshold is not, in this sense, another thing with respect to the limit; it is, so to speak, the experience of the limit itself, the experience of being-within an outside."[11] Why strive to enclose it?

Envisioned as the unequalled space of
correspondence, the threshold calls up
the terror of intimacy – "la présence
irrémissible du moi à soi-même"[12], – and
its irreversibility. It is the multiplied
instant of our apprehension and our
disappearance. It is in this interstice that
the everything that remains just(ly) out of
reach conjugates itself by falling to pieces
– *en dérapant* (by slipping away) – while
wanting to be both here and elsewhere.
"Tout est; rien n'est. L'une et l'autre
formule apportent une égale sérénité.
L'anxieux, pour son malheur, reste entre
les deux, tremblant et perplexe, toujours
à la merci d'une nuance, incapable
de s'établir dans la sécurité de l'être
ou de l'absence de l'être."[13] *L'anxieux*
might be the writer who goes toward
the undecidable – threshold, rooftop,
dérapage. Writing, envisioned thus, must
reach toward such freedoms; it must risk
itself, risk its language – and the forms in
which it tends to want to enclose itself –

to the point, if need be, of suicide.

§

How does the space of potentiality, of possible freedom, end up subtracting itself categorically from life (*la vie*) to give itself over, if only provisionnally, to the void (*le vide*)? Whether it is "l'inconvénient d'être né", or "la tristeza de lo que nace"[14], the necessarily interrupted reach brings about an unachievable return toward a banished place : indeed, the place of writing, overthrown by the very words that would engender it, by those scorchings that manifest themselves brutally in "la chair incrustée dans la parole".[15]

Writing engages in all of these senses, deploying itself every which way in pre-established (disintegrating)[16] mental and urban circuitries, the (provisional, threatened) body offering itself as an agglomeration, a breathless gathering

of parts and counter-parts, of time and
untimeliness, riveted, felled, bursting,
liquid. When it arrives, serene or
desperate, at the upward moments of
building, those rooftops which I have
not done praising – but praise always in
the form of a trial (an essay), an attempt,
a grope, seduction and surge – it is only
just beginning : it reaches. Still, reach
entails the very real risk of collapse : what
assembles itself in the immaculate field
of vision is stained with constructions
leading nowhere if not : elsewhere. The
field of vision, the empty field because
empty of who is seeing, is the field (the
fear?) of death. To enter a text in this
way is also to enter forcibly. It is to offer
oneself up to crossings that don't arrive,
other than at the threshold of a gesture
which is no where near accomplished.

Le Corbusier's romantic gloss of Algerian
architecture disallows the body to situate
itself : it is without subject, subjugated.

The emptying out he undertakes brings about the execution of movement, of correspondence, in the exact place where it might otherwise find formulation. Where the terraces open onto the sea, they are decisevely *terrassées*. The ocular occupation of the open ensures its delineation, its sublimation, its arrest.

When Pizarnik declares : "He dado el salto de mí al alba. / He dejado mi cuerpo junto a la luz", she gives herself to liquid air, the affective area of the tome, of the anticipated tomb, the priviledged space of literature : that of suicide. The movement toward dawn, surge of hopefulness and capitulation, decorates her with vanquished luminosity. She concludes : "y he cantado la tristeza de lo que nace."[17] The sadness of what is born from all arrested time. This text in three truncated movements which opens a book,[18] opens while closing, granting itself, body and reach, to a light that returns, to the

opaque gesture of ending, its disguised
transparency.

Such is the wager – and the lure – of
the unoccupied open, and of the
threshold which leads there. The
space (the rooftop) which offers itself
as empty swallows up what it can of
life, makes itself uninhabitable. The
promising threshold of overreached limits
denies access to a fragile elsewhere. *Le
dérapage* paradoxically prolongs its cry
of deliverance. The surroundings, at all
time visible, palpable to the eyes, melt
into fugitive timelessness, melt into
imperceptible, solicited, disabused masses.
What takes itself for granted (a name, a
city) grants nothing, or else everything
at once: either way, the result is its
disappearance, its incessant reformulation.
For the occupation of the rooftop, the
situation of the body at those upward
moments of building can only occur in
flashes, and by illumination. The space

of potentiality is also the frantic space
of death, whose presence is everywhere
announced. Its defeat is contingent on
the risk required of whoever dares lean a
body into an endlessly falsified opening.
The "livre erreur", then, is at every instant
on the verge of disappearing, on an
implacable edge summoned by a discourse
of recuperation. To remove the body from
the instant is also to enclose it away from
the gesture that might liberate it, is to
inflict the violence of nomination, "une
violence que nous faisons aux choses", or
at very least "une pratique que nous leur
imposons."[19] It is to occupy the space
that calls the body to it; it is to refuse the
pliable architecture of possibility.

§

The relationship between thought
and ruin entails a linguistic collapse :
"Whichever word you speak – / you owe /
to destruction."[20] The irrecuperable debt,

clumsily accommodated by the mouth
that speaks it is ceaselessly reversed in the
obliterated space from which it emerges,
a shard continually reappropriated and
abandoned. The dimension of abandon is
inscrutable. The part of the self promised
to the past which holds it is the part
that is, at least affectively, suppressed.
Speaking confines, distances; speaking
formidable frivolity. Celan speaks well
his era, and those to come, when he
declares of the (spoken) present and of
destruction (announced in speaking) : the
devastated terrain of literature is that of
our expectations, and of our execution.
The desire to piece it into an approachable
sense, to constitute it into a coherent
form betrays an underlying desire for
absolutism. When form incoheres, it
oversteps its own suspected (certainly
suspect) lines, committing textual
suicide.[21]

The "organized violence committed

on ordinary speech"[22] spills outside of the limits of so-called language, manifesting itself in the degradation of structural materiality – ordinary objects manipulated into elusive form. In the case of sculptor Eva Hesse, her abstract pieces reveal themselves to be friable, inconveniently decomposing in the dwellings of her collectors – dwellings that appear to be impermeable, but whose atmospheric interaction with the works lead to their untimely disintegration; exhausted, inexhaustible breath of material and subtle correspondences, fortuitous and crumbling. Hesse frames herself in an accessory dilemma. She leans formally and sensibly against the grid as "both a prison and a safeguard".[23] Paradoxical reach, therefore, whose restrained, girded force, is walled into tensional elasticity, threatening at every moment the hermeticism of limits whose transgression (willed or unwilled) underhandedly manifests itself through

(mindless) states of compositional
degradation : what, of the body, appears
to remain intact, becomes undone when
it comes into contact with unsuspected
influences that are nonetheless anticipated
by the material itself. Thus does language
maintain an embattled, productive
relationship to form, spilling precariously
over an edge of being into a relational
void.

§

The precarious reach – withheld or
consummated – is the fugitive desire that
desires without respite and satiatedly;
is the body volatilised by the call that
orients it and the end that disclaims it.
Do we dare affirm, with Derrida, that
this desire "avait lieu, son lieu, entre cet
appel et cette menace?" And in addition:
"Qu'attendait-il?"[24] A call both silenced
and reinvested with the desire that tugs
at it, distended by the echo that comes

immediately to claim it, threatening the hermeticism in which it indulges, that is the voice by which it is provisionally constituted. Voice-of-nothingness, according to Nina Bouraoui, for "elle s'échappe comme du vent." [25] The place of escape – the breach – reveals itself to be the place of every enclosure, mouths shut and hands tied, of surveyed spaces. The installation of the void anticipates the reach that will distinguish itself, and the city, its humiliation. Between the eyes and the open, there is : arrest. There is : unrest.

§

Certainly, the circumscriptions undertaken against the body in suspense, seized and rerouted, melt themselves, fold into and detach from the architectures at their heels, refuting and delineating. Sensitive and rebarbative, these constructions stalk and stray, and possibility is disputed along their lines, at the very place of refusal, which opens violently to the unexpected. Arrest-unrest is accomplished in disintegration, in the incessant interruption of reconstitutions. Desire  for movement, coagulated and sated. The body envisioned thus is augmented by a declaration of intent, retrieved at the place of its infractions, of which we are … a part.[26]

Strange assemblage of mortuary and juridical lexicons. Wanting to appropriate the sea for the colonising population, Le Corbusier develops, in 1932-1934, a plan whose name is unambiguous – the Plan Obus – whose curvilinear viaduct was to imitate the trajectory of an exploding shell.[27] This plan would be occluded in favour of other, subsequent plans that would replace or modify this one, but its effects nonetheless cast a shadow, if only symbolically, on the upward moments of fantasised building.

§

Planification urbaine, intervention chirurgicale. Les grands travaux *de Haussmann, les* sventramenti *de Mussolini, le Plan Voisin de Le Corbusier. Haussmann se vante d'avoir détruit 19 722 maisons à Paris, dont 4 300 dans la vieille cité. L'éventrement urbain n'a pas à chercher loin son analogue affectif. La nomination, se voulant elle-même monumentale, rase ce qui reste du moi, ses derniers effectifs, sa personne –* inconnue. *Le 21 novembre 2007, dans un mail adressée à Michael O'Leary : "[…] this surgical procedure of disembowelment as applied to cities seems to me entirely related to this question of art; the figure is delineative; delineation is systematic, fixed; what the sventramenti did was to collapse everything into one devastated pit. I think that we have not emerged from it yet."* ²⁸

An affective detour : In the familial imaginary, Claude Cohen (1938-1946), son of Louisa (1908-), dead in Oran just after the birth of Francine (1945-), occupies the space of unmarred potentiality, and of historical, communal martyrdom, a cypher for a kind of affective devastation; as with any telling or transmission, the language used to mark Claude's memory is a language of inevitable imprisonment, for the force of its potentiality lies precisely in the impossibility for him to consume, let alone consummate it. To speak, as it were, a name other than the one attributed to him. To this dual imposition – dual, because it is imposed by heritage, but also because I inflict a framework on it, albeit one that is continually, and deliberately, dismantled – is harnessed the question of place and lodging, that is whether "ç'aurait été sur les lieux mêmes de la déchéance qu'il aurait fallu habiter…"²⁹ Deliberately razed or subject to inclement weather, the disintegrated imprint of these places anticipates the gazes that will attempt to surround them. Whether spaces of habitation or of passage, they carry the same risk. Their temporality is deployed in defferal. "Je suis déjà là-haut, sous le vaste ciel: libre presque."³⁰ It is this "presque" (almost) which disturbs the space of threatened freedom. Which pulls the body between arrest and unrest, between emptiness (the free-fall between the walls of the Casbah) and the law (of the territory).

§

That the open is exacerbated by arrest; that unrest regulates, by its threats, the rooftop where arrest makes its appeal : so be it. But its disintegration, whether due to inclement weather or the forces of order, which entails and anticipates

made and un-made forms, imposed and
discredited lineages, reigns in a place
that is not intermediary, but in a space of
reiterative ending. It is neither between,
nor outside, but is accomplished in defeat,
in dismemberment, in infinite finitude.
Our part – our apartness – is the residual
that escapes the remains which, in turn,
escape it. It discovers and devastates
in the very place of possibility – where
everything *dérape*, including possibility
itself, which launches and dislodges, stirs
and expires.

§

*Forte de ses forteresses, la pensée s'organise
en dépit des obstructions, des saillies et
étonnements qui l'entravent – ou justement
à cause d'eux. Le traumatisme du langage
est la gageure même de nos correspondances
– de nos corps répondants. Corps incertains
constitués d'éructations, de grossières
gesticulations, de lambeaux de nausées, de*

faiblissements, tous appuyés contre un même verbiage. La consolation serait un leurre mis en place pour pallier à l'inattendue dévastation, pourtant anticipée.[31]

It is quite possible that the promising eventuality of the rooftop which grants access to the open, to a (material) possibility always within sight, on the verge of being specified, is contingent on the absence of an event. That the upward moments of building may well open all passages, on the condition that none be taken. For the unexpected need not reside in the suicidal gesture proposed by these rooftops[32] – abandonment to the seductive void, to the fragile guarantees of sublime dawns – nor need it reside in the appropriation of the space as an apprehended dwelling. But in the consciousness of our own advent … suspended by every place that precedes us. It is an error to believe that it is even possible to inhabit a space. To see in

potentiality the seat of some (named or
unnamed) power. What, of the flagellated
present escapes us, at the contested
limits of writing, is the trembling body
reconstituted in keeping with its own
disappearance, for every utterance is a
provisional utterance. Such that what is
open remains necessarily open.

§

In the tormented logic of the architecture
of this essay[33], the passage from rooftop
to the open is not of course without
difficulty or distortion. If current
history and past history remind us
that "…nous vivons l'échappatoire,
l'échappatoire c'est moi,"[34] we cannot,
with a clear conscience, choose enclosure.
Systematisation participates of this
enclosure.[35] By seeking to justify itself
through artificial lineages, by seeking to
give itself a name that will precede it in
its reiterated coming to the world, writing

anticipates itself by gagging itself. Because language will always already have spoken in its place.

So it is that I have difficulty justifying recourse to outmoded compartmentalising categories, specifically, though not exclusively, as they act on writing, that is, as they reduce it, temper it, domesticate it – territorialising themselves in ways surprisingly evocative of colonialism, the same colonialism that puts words in the mouths of those who already know how to speak. For the good children of some nation or other, the nationalist-imperialist reflex is a (latent) motivation which seems to want to renew (gentrify) itself of late – even in the most ostensibly innovative of circles – and with verve.[36] Rather than sink deeper into the debate, I prefer to remain anachronistically seated on the edge of an old rooftop in the company of a young boy dead in Oran in 1946 at the age of eight in the most dubious of circumstances:

« *Claude naît. Cela est certain. Claude naît sur un toit de maison parmi les oiseaux. Sous un ciel maraudeur. L'année des disparitions. L'année des morts fluviales. Et des cabales ferroviaires. L'année où les oiseaux s'envolent définitivement. Avec au bec un petit drapeau de chair.* »[37]

Chicago or elsewhere,
July 2007 – March 2008

1. N.S., *Carnet de désaccords*. ("Berlin, I imagined as much, but I too like not knowing. For the city to be nowhere and elsewhere at the same time." So B. means Berlin when he writes "this city". In July as at every other moment of the year, "this city" only materialises in the splayed space between two letters. This space is as vast and unfathomable as the sea beds and as narrow as a rivulet. "This city" is, of course, neither Berlin nor Lisbon, and locatable on no map, but takes form between two bodies writing one another across the inimitable distance of a friendship. These openings – these breaches – are particular to writing; intimacy opened onto a world caught off guard.) Translations are my own, unless indicated otherwise. All subsequent epigraphic passages are from the *Carnet de désaccords*. Montréal, Le Quartanier, 2009.

2. That Heideggerian elsewhere evoked by Simone de Beauvoir. "L'homme est un être des lointains." *Pour une morale de l'ambiguïté suivi de Pyrrhus et Cinéas*, Paris, Gallimard, 1947 / 1944, p. 219.

3. *L'absence au lieu (Claude Cahun et le livre inouvert)*, Québec, Nota Bene, coll. "Nouveaux essais Spirale," 2007.

4. *...s'arrête? Je*, Montréal, Éditions de L'Hexagone, 2007, p. 47. ("Je prends le livre erreur de l'étagère et le mets sur le sol. C'est ainsi que je dispose de ce souvenir particulier. Sait-on jamais ? Il se loge dans la hanche les jours trempés. Il affame les parties tendres. La gorge s'élance dans la bouche et bloque. Alors je l'avale en moi. // Je bois l'eau d'une tasse rouillée. // Je pleus avec le ciel. // Je pleus de la poussière.")

5. If I say that I write l'entre-genre, it need not

(necessarily) follow that I reject poetry, or philosophy, or the essay, or narrative, but locate myself at the disreputable and misunderstood place where they touch, that is, in the multiple breaches that result from their more or less violent encounters, in the present (presence) of their ceaselessly renewed expression.

6. *(We learn nothing from buildings by limiting ourselves to a study of their facades – their doors, windows, and walls. Their frameworks (wood, metal, vinyl) and their coverage (stucco, aluminium, brick, stone, or plaster). Openings and coverings. Transparency and subterfuge. Closure and bravado. During my first visit to Chicago, buildings presented themselves to me otherwise; they offered me a new sense, an unexpected form of approach. By their rooftops. That is something worth thinking about. Having lived in cities which priviledge underground public transit, I wasn't expecting my vision of a city to be overthrown by the simple fact of an elevated rail that follows its centenial course at the same height as, and sometimes above, the buildings of a large number of residential neighbourhoods. Thus is exposed the most intimate aspect of a building : its covering.)*

7. Zeynep Çelik, "Gendered Spaces in Colonial Algiers," *The Sex of Architecture*, eds Diana Agrest, et al., New York, Harry N. Abrams, Inc., Publishers, 1996, p. 130.

8. Le Corbusier, "Un exemple de folklore architectural: La Casbah d'Alger," *Voici la France de ce mois*, vol. 3, no. 28 (September 1942), p. 14. ("...for from each dwelling, from the terrace – and this accretion of terraces appears as a sort of magic staircase

descending toward the sea – we see space, the sea.").
9. Walter Benjamin, "On Language as Such and on the Language of Man," *Reflections*, trans. Edmund Jephcott, New York, Schocken Books, 1978, p. 327.
10. Sketch by Charles Brouty, in Lucienne Favre, *Tout l'inconnu de la Casbah d'Alger*, Alger, Bacconier Frères, 1933, p. 253.
11. Giorgio Agamben, *The Coming Community*, trans. Michael Hardt, Minneapolis/London, Minnesota University Press, 1993, p. 69.
12. Emmanuel Lévinas, *De l'évasion*, Paris, Fata Morgana, 1982, 113. ("The self's intolerable presence to the self." trans. Bettina Bergo).
13. Cioran, *De l'inconvénient d'être né*, Paris, Gallimard, 1973, p. 14. ("*Everything is. Nothing is*. One and other bring equal serenity. The anxious person, for his misfortune, remains between the two, trembling and confused, always at the mercy of a nuance, incapable of establishing himself in the security of being or the absence of being.")
14. Alejandra Pizarnik, *Poesía completa*, Barcelona, Editorial Lumen, 2000, p. 103. ("The sadness of what is born")
15. Danielle Collobert, *Oeuvres I,* Paris, POL, 2005, p. 411. ("its flesh […] inlaid in speech", trans. Norma Cole).
16. "Commencer à penser, c'est commencer d'être miné", Albert Camus, *Le mythe de Sispyhe*, Paris, Gallimard, 1942, p. 17. ("Beginning to think is beginning to be undermined." trans. Justin O'Brien).
17. "I gave the surge of myself to the dawn. / I joined my body to the light / and sang the sadness of what is born."

18. *El arból de Diana.*

19. Michel Foucault, *L'ordre du discours*, Paris, Gallimard, 1971, p. 55. ("We must conceive discourse as *a violence we do to things*, or in any case as *a practice which we impose on them*."trans. Ian Mcleod. Emphases correspond with phrases implanted in the text above.)

20. Paul Celan, as quoted by John Felstiner in *Paul Celan: Poet, Survivor, Jew,* New Haven and London, Yale University Press, 1995.

21. "[…] literature is like a deadly weapon with which language commits suicide." Todorov, cited by Terence Hawkes in *Structuralism and Semiotics*, Berkeley and Los Angeles, University of California Press, 1977, p. 106.

22. Viktor Erlich quoting Jakobson, as cited by Terence Hawkes, *op. cit.*, p. 71.

23. "Hesse used the grid as both a prison and a safeguard against letting an obsessive process or excessive sensitivity run away with her." Lucy Lippard, *Eva Hesse*, New York, Da Capo Press, p. 209.

24. Jacques Derrida, *Feu la cendre*, Paris, des femmes, 1987 / 1998, p. 9. ("…had a place, its place, between this desire and this risk? What was it waiting for?" *Cinders*, trans. Ned Lukacher, University of Nebraska Press, 1991, p. 23.)

25. Nina Bouraoui, *Garçon manqué,* Paris, Stock, 2000, p. 132. ("…it escapes like the wind.")

26. Image: Algiers, 1935 (aerial view, where the casbah (right) and the French quarters (left) correspond). In Le Corbusier, *La Ville Radieuse: Éléments d'une doctrine d'urbanisme pour l'équipement de la civilisation machiniste*, Paris, Éditions Vincent, Fréal & Cie, p. 230.

27. Zeynep Çelik, *Urban forms and Colonial Confrontations : Algiers under French Rule*, Berkeley and L.A./ London, University of California Press, 1997, p. 76. With much ado to Rachel Gontijo Araújo for circling with me around these and other questions, bodies, texts.

28. *(Urban planning, surgical intervention. The* grands travaux *of Haussmann, the* sventramenti *of Mussolini, the* Plan Voisin *of Le Corbusier. Haussman takes pride in having destroyed 19,722 houses in Paris, 4,300 of which are in the old part of the city. Urban disembowelement needn't look far for its affective counterpart. Nomination, wishing itself monumental, razes the rest of me, its last effects, its* unknown *person. November 21, 2007, in a letter addressed to Michael O'Leary : "[…] this surgical procedure of disembowelment as applied to cities seems to me entirely related to this question of art; the figure is delineative; delineation is systematic, fixed; what the* sventramenti *did was to collapse everything into one devastated pit. I think that we have not emerged from it yet.")*

29. Assia Djebar, *La disparition de la langue française*, Paris, Albin Michel, 2003, p. 69. ("…it would have been necessary to live on the very sites of decline.")

30. *Ibid.*, p. 157. ("I am already up there, beneath the vast sky : free, almost.")

31. *("By the force of its fortresses, thought organizes itself despite obfuscating obstructions, surges and surprises – or perhaps because of them. The trauma of language is the very wager of our correspondences – of our "corps répondants". Bodies of uncertainty made of*

belches and vile gesticulations, shreds of nausea, weaknesses, each leaning into one and the same verbiage. Consolation might be a lure put in place to soften the unexpected, but nonetheless anticipated, devastation.")
32. After all, "le suicide, comme le saut, est l'acceptation à sa limite." Albert Camus, *op. cit.*, p. 77. ("Suicide, like the leap, is acceptance at its extreme." trans. Justin O'Brien).
34. *L'absence au lieu (Claude Cahun et le livre inouvert), op. cit.*, p. 41. ("…we are living the breach, the breach is me.")
35. The twentieth century has unfurled the fatal consequences of an extreme, if not extremist expression of rational systematisation (the Sho'ah, Hiroshima, Cambodia, Iraq these days, and so on), and our current cultural tendencies participate far and near in this systematisation, raising the spectres of the most suspect and troublesome of motivations.
36. Well over a century ago, (1892), Paul Valéry broke with poetry as a form, André Gide refused, with one exception, the term 'novel' (*Les faux-monnayeurs*, which hardly resembled what passed for a novel at the time) rejecting poetry as well; more recently, the texts of Jeanne Hyvrard (which she terms "réalités") take their own distance from the usual categories, only to situate themselves where they happen to be, that is, mid-way between several genres at once. Édouard Glissant writes an essay (*L'intention poétique*) more akin to prose poetry, and these are but a few examples culled from a near-extinguished movement away from the safe constructs / constraints of genre.
37. *("Claude is born. That much is certain. Claude is*

born on a rooftop among birds. Beneath a marauding sky. The year of the disappearances. The year of the effluvial deaths. And the railway cabals. The year during which the birds fly off for good. With a small flag of flesh in their beaks.")

CORRESPONDANCES
Montréal … Chicago … Wherever

IT IS POSSIBLE TO WRITE *one's day through letters, a letter.*[1]

N … Je ne te promets rien. Viens, je te ferai voir. L'erreur est de vouloir saisir l'insaisissable. De projeter sur une ville, n'importe laquelle, le fardeau de ses espoirs, d'attribuer au désir une topographie trop particulière, d'en tracer les sillons comme s'il s'agissait de veiner sa destinée, d'y injecter le pouls d'une certaine dérive, d'en faire un délire magistral, tu vois où je veux en venir : de la nommer. De nommer les rues, les ruines, les épaves, les caniveaux,

les canaux, les squares, les routes, les
chemins, les parcs. D'en escalader les
pentes, de déraper sur les pavés moites
de sa réputation surfaite; pourtant tu ne
l'as pas inventée, elle est palpable, elle
t'a séduite, envahie, désolée. J'en bois,
moi, tous les matins, penchée sur l'écume
suspecte du Saint-Laurent, depuis la
rive parsemée de tessons de bouteilles et
d'une patrouille surchauffée, depuis la rue
Willibrord le dimanche des Rameaux et
des cris condamnant les Juifs d'avoir tué le
dieu périmé de ce bord. Les permissions,
vois-tu, vont de main en main avec les
refoulements, la libération coûte cher, on
ne sait plus trop de quoi on se défait. On
convie à la défaite … N

*What I first saw was monumental. A
saillie of gorgeous concrete. Stairs spiralling.
Turrets. A rue piétonne. Pigeons shitting on
cobbled walks. A joie de vivre? It is best not
to dream too much.*

N … Je ne voudrais point t'en dissuader, mais je te préviens, tu seras appelée à te situer. Un jour ou l'autre on l'exigera de toi, tu verras que tes langues entières cesseront de fonctionner. Tu fais mieux, là où tu iras, de vivre en étrangère. Curieuse anfractuosité du terrain langagier. Au point où j'en suis, je voudrais qu'on puisse l'aborder autrement. Dire du lieu : comble, plutôt que manquement. Anciennement j'écrivais *ni l'une, ni l'autre, et toutes deux à la fois.* Et bien plus tard, *à peu près nulle part.* Je veux en venir à ce vide, qui n'est ni d'ici, ni d'hier, mais qui s'est étendu sur toute ma littérature en débarquant ici – pourtant j'y suis née, c'est, ce sont, mes langues. Dire ici, tout comme dire mes langues, c'est entretenir une certitude que je n'ai pas. C'est malmener la vérité. Surtout c'est vouloir repérer une écriture polylogue dans un lieu scindé. L'y arrimer. Du reste, cette conversation n'aurait lieu nulle part ailleurs, je pense; pourtant on n'est pas en manque, sur ce continent, de nationalismes. Je n'aurais pas justement à te dire « Viens mais. » Je te dirais « Viens » tout court et tu viendrais … N

Because bastards ululate on Saint-Denis at midnight, moon or no moon. And I ululate with them. With my scarf tight around my throat, mamzer. And my dogs cowering because they don't like to see me like this. With my mouth wrapped around a sound, cabrón, I am incapable of making.

N … Imagine un peu que tes deux langues soient des langues frontières. Que l'une te renvoie à l'autre mais qu'aucune ne soit véritablement habitable. Que tu sois lue en fonction de ce dédoublement et que le résultat en soit non un d'abondance mais de recul. Ce qui a la propension à s'illimiter, à se répandre, à s'élargir et à se transformer, en vient à devenir le signifiant d'une limite totalisante, si ce n'est totalitaire. C'est dire que chacune d'elles, et donc toi, puisque tu y es prise, sinon éprise, agit comme un atoll, comme un fait hermétique isolant l'une dans l'autre. Peu importe que tu sois dans ton anglais à Montréal ou dans ton français à Toronto, l'effet sur tes textes en est un de défaite, et non de fête, car, et pourquoi, le tout est malencontreusement brimé par une « surfaite » de méfiance sublimée qui travaille doucement ses expulsions – de part et d'autre. D'où ton penchant pour le nulle-part. Un choix véritable, une situation, mais qui t'a toutefois été inculquée. Ta philosophie en est une élaborée dans la nécessité, et depuis ce terrain vague tu arrives malgré tout à te tailler une place ... déplacée. Insituable. On te l'a maintes fois fait remarquer. Tu résistes farouchement à l'incorporation, tu ne demandes aucune permission, tu évites de t'installer. Tu en arrives à ce constat : que ta disposition linguistique, qui fait de toi ta provenance contestée, se heurte à un dispositif

administratif dont le souci premier, tu
t'en rends bêtement compte – loin de
mener, ouvrir, poursuivre, accommoder
un dialogue intelligent autour des langues
et des littératures –, est avant tout un
souci dont est soustrait l'élément animal,
c'est-à-dire humain, sensoriel, mouvant,
et même parfois ému, qui passe et repasse
sur un terrain délimité sans aucun égard
pour l'impact des confins aléatoirement
imposés qui, malgré toi, s'érigent dans
ton sommeil dans de hideux complexes
bureaucratiques, qui d'une main te
convoitent, et de l'autre raturent ce qui
sort de ta bouche manuscrite… N

*This is the things with tenses. Their
governance and the insolence of our lives.
Say: What was. Will have been. I mark the
spot X and rub the ground hard until the X
disappears. It only disappears insofar as it is
not visible to those who did not put it there.
As for me, it is in me and I see it always and
anyway I needn't because it is there.*

N … Je voudrais en revenir à ces langues frontières, aux contrôles arbitraires qui font que l'on se lance, avec fougue, et sans trop de réticence, dans cette conversation. Les balises sont, dirait-on, prédisposées. On parle, pour ainsi dire, du fonds d'un puits où l'eau a cessé, depuis longtemps, de couler, et dans l'étanchéité et l'oubli total de la porosité, le refus d'une certaine géographie, alors que notre champ de vision est arbitrairement figé. J'en arrive à me dire que l'imposition d'une certaine identification (quelle qu'elle soit – linguistique, sexuelle, culturelle…) oblige à l'entretien d'un rapport précis à l'état, borné par l'état, qui artificialise la relation dont il se dépêche de s'absenter, de s'abstenir. Ce qui me mène à provoquer une série de dislocations dans cette matière (architecturale car maniée) qui obéit aux principes d'un univers somme toute inventé. J'en considère la malléabilité, la porosité, et en arrive à des reformulations éventuellement extra-étatiques (et pas forcément extra-politiques ou -politisées), extra-géographiques, une sorte de reconstitution deleuzienne de l'espace langagier, stratifié, tendre, c'est-à-dire ouvert. À la place des langues frontières, je conçois des langues embrasures (embrasées), ouvertures, brèches, césures, dans le matériau de la littérature, des lieux de passage, d'entrée, d'accès, des seuils langagiers qui viendraient bouleverser la fermeture de la frontière sans en oblitérer l'existence. Je passe. Je sais que je passe. Je passe à travers. Je me retourne. Le passage ne se referme pas derrière moi. Il y a la trace laissée par mes pas. Là. Tu me rejoins. On cause … N

The cities fold over and over. Union Square shows up at the foot of Montjuïc. The Chicago River cuts a path across Dartmoor. And the Orio stops at the foot of St. Denis.

N … Tant de réticence. Je ne voudrais
jamais devoir nommer. Dire ici à Chicago.
Ici à Montréal. Ici là-bas où je suis, ai
été. Vois-tu. J'en viens à me reconnaître
dans les lieux dont je disparais. Subsiste
une trace, des traces dans les endroits
que j'ai quittés. Je me rends compte que
finalement je n'ai quitté nulle part, ce qui
m'est étourdissant à ingérer : une pluralité
de moi, dont je ne suis plus responsable,
et que je suis incapable de repêcher des
endroits où je les ai abandonnés. Le
lieu se déplie, s'étale, se superpose sur
l'autre, avant, après. Je voudrais te confier
cette expérience bien particulière du
mouvement, en adoucir la barbarie, car il
y a violence dans l'acte d'ouvrir la bouche
sur un lieu bien précis, de le nommer et
d'en attendre quelque chose, puis le fuir,
en être chassée. C'est toi que j'attends
bien entendu, au bout de la ligne, au
tournant de la page. Fuyante – mais quoi,
la langue, la page, toi… On est troquée
contre sa nationalité (ses nationalités). On

est troquée contre sa langue. Contre sa capacité de résister. On dit reste, tu seras récompensée. On dit le lieu d'où tu viens mais ce n'est pas vrai. On dit qui tu es mais on n'en sait rien. On dit le lieu où tu es c'est tout ce qu'on connaît. On dit myope. On dit blindé. On dit tais-toi. On dit bouge pas. On dit jamais. La langue se referme sur les lettres qu'on écrirait, que je t'écrirais. Car au fond, finalement, que tu sois ici ou là-bas, tu écriras. À Chicago on te dira Canada. À Toronto on te dira Montréal. À Montréal Lyon. À London America. À Barcelone France. On te dira n'importe quoi. On fera en fonction. On fera une fonction de toi. Tellement on veut traquer le mouvement des corps qu'on en oublie ses lettres. Peu importe que tu te retires : toi, comment te lirais-je? Quand la littérature a-t-elle cessé d'être contestataire? De remettre en question son milieu? De s'imposer malgré le risque couru? À présent qu'elle se referme sur elle-même, on en est à se demander quel gouvernement elle sert. Quelle frontière elle protège. Quel mythe elle entretient. Et de quel droit? Passe à côté. Refuse le lieu, le lieu te refuseras. Va à la rencontre de ce qui attend ... N.

                      Chicago, mai 2006

1. Transcribed passages are all from *The Sorrow And The Fast Of It* (Cold Spring: Nightboat Books, 2007).

FROM ASTRAY TO ESTRANGED
(SELF-)TRANSLATING CLAUDE CAHUN

THE BODY ESTRANGED IS ESTRANGED
in *The City, estrangement being a function
of The City; it is incapable of maintaining a
distinction before The City which it becomes,
to which it is assimilated. Consequently, The
City, itself a* corpus, *acts on the body that
traverses it similarly. The inside is absorbed
into the outside, one is but the exposition of
the other; despite themselves, body and City
end up speaking to one another, arguing,
struggling with each other : space (here) is at
stake. One and other are meeting places and
touch with malice, discontent and delight.*

Estrangement corresponds *with The City.*

It might be the means by which one would approach the other, for The City approaches the body as much as the opposite occurs. I would go so far as to say that one is the other, one is an integral (bodily) part of the other. Its limbs, its words, its gestures and exhalations exist in relation *to the gutters, sewers, scaffoldings and masonery. The City is the body's scaffolding, just as the body furnishes the scaffolding for the book as it is written. A confused, tilted, twisted scaffolding, no doubt, but implicated nonetheless. This observation is not only of a symbolic order; The City, which is concomitantly akin to the monument and the scrap, is a presence, and to say presence is to say consequence. It is the consequence of a labour, of hand work. It is the consequence of a convergence, in one place, of several bodies and historical moments, of violence and voluptuousness, of desire and ravages, of distrust and regret. To say City is to say feat and defeat, to say encounter, to say body and rise, metal and*

*fall. The bodies, agglomerated into a City,
leave their imprints, which return to us
as we move through it. The raised wall,
the suspended bridge, the poured tarmac,
come, with assured displacement, from
ourselves. Estrangement, manifest as much
physically (the physicality of The City, of
the body that moves along its avenues) as
it is psychologically (affective estrangement,
a sort of dissociation, disjuncture of the
senses) might be the result of this dislocation,
the oblivion that surfaces (in) us and
through which we recall what, of the city,
disappeared, enters us by these (di)versions.
(Di)versions that we effect and undertake
by clearing, by deciphering (always
ephemerally) the momentous moment that
fixes and wrenches with its grinding work,
and where the present takes place with
persistent displacement.*[1]

It was no accident. It was altogether
unexpected. Let alone the aleatory
convergences that made a book of a

sentence, uttered carelessly into the ear of someone who happened to be listening. For the book to have run away with me. For the book to have led me astray.

There was the concurrence of circumstance and correspondence. The cities were not negligible in this instance either, and each did its business for me, and at times seditiously. In Montréal there was a channel leading to a small green room at the front of a ground floor apartment in Chicago, facing away from a garden; and its offshoots, toward Brooklyn, Soho, Iowa City, the Wrigley Building, and more latently, toward Lyon, Nantes, Paris and the Isle of Jersey, each of whose currents drew and withdrew inferences. A catalogue of absences. First, the small animal at my feet. And those, more obvious. Claude Cahun's for example, and the language – the other language – that walled me in to her-him.

The book is of course, *Écrits*, the near-
exhaustive collection of Cahun's writings,
assembled by her biographer, François
Leperlier.[2] It is also *L'absence au lieu.*[3] It is
Absence Where As.[4] Which is it?
To take a photograph as a place of
willful departure. There is nothing
willful about it. (Or else yes, sure, with
departure anticipating its own omission,
its own admission.) Rather, there is the
incident of looking, which opens the
body unexpectedly to manifestations
of its self in an other. An other who
simultaneously projects and ingests you
against it, reiteratively mechanising a
moment of encounter, across time –
Montréal, then Chicago, 2006; Paris,
1936 – only to disperse it redundantly;
and with each iteration, some small,
unaccountable adjustment is made,
such that the dispersal, arisen from that
moment of encounter – of resemblance
– collapses one into other, locking itself
into an endless reissuance of the self

through disappearance. In each instance, leaving something behind, of myself, of Cahun, of the thing caught between us. Desire, some might say. And perhaps even residually, translation, a breach.

Willful or unwilled, these are translative instances of disobedience. Of collision and collusion. Of fastidious upheaval. What complicates this particular gesture is the (inter-)mixing of selves, the synchronous compression into one body of several, and their, its, dissemination, through language of one and the same, multiplied, derailed.

All this time we are seated – she is in fact she is standing – Claude Cahun and I, so to speak, across from one another. The resemblance is troubling. And this for several reasons. First, this resemblance, whether imagined or real, presupposes a memory that does not exist, that cannot exist. I don't remember her. I have no reason to

remember her. Because it happens that
we are very distinctly indistinct she and I.
*This resemblance is not only physiological;
it goes far beyond the lines of the face,
the nature of the gaze, the sensibility
projected from the photograph. There are
the biographical details, Cahun's ideological
engagement, her artistic contribution, her
judeity, even the fragility of her health. There
is also the fact of the French language, and
England. Some might take comfort in such
proximity, a narrative from which to enlarge
one's own. This is not at all my experience.
On the contrary. I feel dread verging on
madness.*

*How can I put it? In her, I resemble myself.
Not : I recognise myself. But resemble
myself. There is no longer distinction,
but indistinction. There is no longer
differentiation, nor even difference, but
absorption. Even more – or less – than this,
there is subtraction, and not accumulation
as one might think, subtraction of one from*

the other, subtraction that results in the erasure, the nullification of the two of us.

The photograph offers itself as an abyss.[5]

The claim I make to (self-)translation is the claim Claude Cahun has already made of me. *L'absence au lieu* documents that claim. A photographic seizure. Dead time, incessant. The you and the I of it blurred in that moment of resemblance, enabling the turn *into* the thing that drives me away. And I, as it were, many times removed. It is this repetitive removal that the work of *L'absence au lieu* attests to, testifying in the place of the thing that cannot speak for itself. The image, yes. Claude Cahun, less evidently. And time – or historicity – most of all. Over and over, I have described this work as a book of correspondence, an *ethics* of correspondence. In the reach, through letters, toward the dead. There have been Colette, Gide, Cahun. And others,

whose names die on the page, only to die
again. This is most certainly not a text
of resurrection, of resurgence, of stakes
planted firmly in the soil of some fantasy
of renewal, of kinship, of proximity.
It is instead the work of distances and
disappearances, working over body and
text, of unending endings.

I would want to stop at these distances,
at these disappearances, but I cannot. It
is precisely through the (self-)translative
gesture, that I make my appeal, and
that it is repeatedly rejected. By the text
itself, and my willful unwillingness to
be enclosed in the thing that contains
me already, and I it. In the turn from
French to English, the work of time is
altered – *altérée*. What stops short – *dead
time* – in *L'absence au lieu* outlasts itself
in (self-)translation; this is no afterlife, if
anything, it is residue, silt. And let it be
said that what calls itself (self-)translation
is perhaps not translation at all, but

reiteration, or some other thing, and this distinction is an important one, for the body leans differently from language to language, and breaks differently also. At another time, I maintained that translating myself was *one hand breaking itself that redundant.* That the languages in such close proximity cancelled one another out, cancelling the body in keeping with the text, holding nothing where what was is not anymore, or was not ever: ontologically untenable. Precisely because this work belies the possibility of proximity – as does the work of writing. If the time of *L'absence au lieu* was a time of enclosure, of suffocation, the time of *Absence Where As* provided the illusion of travelled distances, of approach, of an outside, perhaps even reachable: the promise and the lure of correspondence. To the days of writing enclosure in French were appended furious moments of rewriting, in the form of letters, short passages for the

most part, excerpts from the manuscript
in production, *in English*, postmarked,
if only virtually, and thus assuring me
of my presence in a place that was and
is continually slipping away from me.
These epistolary moments marked a form
of movement that was not possible at a
desk, in a chair, before a wall, with Cahun
staring back at me, for the duration.
Six weeks, uninterrupted. The work of
language in time, cleaving me from the
place where I was, undermined (if only in
illusion) by the letters sent to those who
could attest to the writing of the book.
Such that this book of correspondence
conceals a subterfuge of correspondence,
in the form of "real" letters, that, while
duplicating the work of the photograph,
acting themselves as invective directed at
me (look at what you've done).

It would nonetheless be misguided to
attempt to map out these trajectories.
Indeed I did name places. The letters

went to Brooklyn, Soho, and Iowa City from Chicago. The manuscript went to Montréal then to Québec City. And there was the insistance of the wall against which the table sits. But these place names and architectural forms (including the form of the book) say nothing of where we, or I, went, was, or might have been.

During an ongoing conversation with a friend who studies fracture mechanics, failure analysis and catastrophe theory, the matter of cycloid curves[6] entered

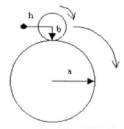

the conversation, leading to a discussion of the workings of philosophy within these disciplines. I should underscore emphatically that I am ignorant of the finer and indeed the brute workings of geometry, non-Euclidian or Euclidian, Riemannian, fractal, algebraic or differential, and so on (I failed grade 8 geometry and decided to leave it at that); but the eloquence of the

line, as it was very elegantly described to
me, and its strange (for me) trajectories
through water or light, between two
points, continue to be productive in
thinking (through) movement and fixity,
correspondence and disjuncture. With
apologies, then, to Michael O'Leary, for
making such distortion of his science, and
insisting on a dislocated application of
thought that may (or may not)[7] prevent a
bridge from collapsing. In correspondence
with Michael last year, I nonetheless
inquired: "Still, the notion of an infinite
number of possible trajectories between
two points begs (for me) the question
of the points and their fixity. Most
immediately, I wonder perplexedly how
on earth this formula might be of use
to you or anyone when the two (fixed)
points are in fact indeterminate – that
is, they will only reveal themselves once
the fracture has occurred, or begun to
occur. So their fixity is contingent on their
having been."[8]

So it is with this task to which I have committed myself, namely the mapping of the movement between *L'absence au lieu* and *Absence Where As*, in which neither text occupies a fixed point, or in which the (moving) points they occupy are not in fixed relationship with one another. Rather than draw up lists of equivalences, I would like to expose a moment of equivocation in the relationship between these two texts – in their own correspondence – evoked in the title of this talk, and the passage from *Absence Where As* with which I opened. And that is how it is I went from *astray* to *estranged*. This sort of equivocation is one I allow myself (and my languages) quite frequently, resisting, even in an essayistic text such as *L'absence au lieu*, the narrow margin of meaning imposed by the choice of certain terms. Or the margin that narrows if a choice is maintained verbatim in the other language. A recent example of this sort of refusal of fixity, within my own thinking, is evident in the ALÉA talks delivered earlier this week. What is developed, in French, as a discussion, part way through the paper, of the terms *attente* and *attentat* (waiting or expectation, and attack, violation, infringement, or assault), are deliberately transposed into English as *arrest* and *unrest*. There is residual evocation of juridical violence (*arrest*) and armed or unarmed resistance (*unrest*) but I reject the powerfully subliminal dictate that requires of me, the writer, that I be loyal to versions of myself.[9]

Certainly, this is evidenced, by now, I think, in my stubbornly equivocal relationship to my names : Nathalie and Nathanaël, which make manifest the insufficiency of language – of desire as it is (mis)pronounced – through the body that makes ambiguous what is required by an overt, and sometimes sublimated, decree to be fixed, in gender, in genre, in relation and formulation (i.e. form). Cock or no cock, as Freud might have it, and in whose pants of course.

Once again, I am leading myself, my selves, astray, into careful disarray. I bring up the question of my names in the context of these (un)certain terms, to underscore their importance for these bodies, these texts. *L'égarement,* like *l'attente*, might be said to be "foundational" to readings of *L'absence* and ALÉA and what become of those texts when they are transposed into texts in which the same "foundational" terms are (mis-)translated as, in this case, *estrangement* (rather than astrayness) and *arrest* (rather than expectation or waiting)? What becomes of the philosophical, epistemic, reliance on foundation, on origination and orderliness,[10] when a text rejects the notion of choice as binaristic, but approaches it as a manifestation of

simultaneity, of accretion, of plurality, of
enlargement of a field of vision or thought
– astray *and* estranged; expectation *and*
arrest – such that these (self-)translations
disallow equivalency or satiation, making
demonstrable the impossibility of
exactitude, security, or equal exchange,
implementing this ontological evidence:
is *and* is-not. Denying the giving-over of
one thing to an other. The strain of this
movement, of this (b)reach, is marked
by a welcome stain. *L'absence au lieu* and
Absence Where As are each contaminated
by the other; they are neither other
nor same. Read together, or apart, they
interact residually, onanistically certainly,
and in keeping with the tensed distances
traversed and left unattempted. There is
some thing and there is always some thing
more. In absence as in avowal.

Claude Cahun *is* and *is-not* Lucy Schwob.
Her (self-)portraits *are* and *are-not*
photographs of him-her. It is in the

hyphen between him and her that gender spins off into its own fluctuant form; it is in the distance between *is* and *is-not* that the death and decay of living things become manifest in language, in the body, before turning toward something else; it is in the space between French and English that my writing body undoes itself from modes of translation, (mis-)pronouncing its own remains, betraying what becomes of me; it is in the distances crossed by the letters that the places change in keeping with the names. We wait for a thing, and when we come upon it, it is already in the process of turning. Such that when we meet, it is always for the first – and last – time.

Chicago, March 2008

1. *Absence Where As (Claude Cahun and the Unopened Book).* New York, Nightboat, 2009.
2. Paris, Jean Michel Place, 1992.
3. Québec, Nota Bene 2007.
4. New York, Nightboat, 2009.
5. From *Absence Where As, op. cit.* Photographs: (Top) Claude Cahun : Vitrine van den Bergh, Launch of *Aveux non avenus*, June 1930 (detail); (Bottom) N / N ; Nathanaël, June 2006.
6. Image borrowed from Hans Mikelson, *Parametric Equation Oscillators.* http://www.csounds.com/ezine/spring1999/synthesis/.
7. The collapse, August 1, 2007, of the Minneapolis I-35W bridge over the Mississippi River (for example).
8. From Michael, in reply: "The cycloid is the optimum path for the brachistochrone problem – how to get from point A to B through a gravity field in the least amount of time. The path of a crack is different. I use the principle of least action to derive the equation of motion of a rapidly propagating crack. The miracle of least action is that you don't specify the end point of the crack in advance. You simply prescribe an arbitrary beginning and an end time to the action – in my case, a crack running along a polyethelyne pipe. So least action is four dimensional. The paths are infinite through the three spatial dimensions, but specified in time. In that sense, least action is a truly predictive principle. It tells you how the crack (or planet or electron or whatever) is going to move by assuming that nature always optimizes. Nature

always chooses the best path. Moreover, least action is the closest thing there is to a unified principle in physics. All of relativity, quantum theory, electricity and magnetism, and mechanics yield their equations of motion through least action." (Private correspondence).

9. This liberty that I grant myself is one I do not take when translating the work of others. The ethical responsibility toward that work is altogether other.

10. Descartes : "Il est vrai que nous ne voyons point qu'on jette par terre toutes les maisons d'une ville, pour le seul dessein de les refaire d'autre façon, et d'en rendre les rues plus belles; mais on voit bien que plusieurs font abattre les leurs pour les rebâtir et que même quelquefois ils y sont contraints, quand elles sont en danger de tomber d'elles mêmes, *et que les fondements n'en sont pas bien fermes.*" (My emphasis). And "Et enfin, comme ce n'est pas assez, avant de commencer à rebâtir un logis où on demeure, que de l'abattre, et de faire provision de matériaux et d'architectes, ou s'exercer soi-même à l'architecture, et outre cela d'en avoir soigneusement tracé le dessin; mais qu'il faut aussi s'être pourvu de quelque autre, où on puisse être logé commodément pendant le temps qu'on y travaillera[…]". *Discours de la méthode suivi des Méditations*, Paris, Union générale d'éditions, 1951, p. 41 and 51 respectively. For an English version, see *The Rationalists: René Descartes, Benedict de Spinoza*, Gottfried Wilhelm Freiherr Von Leibniz, New York, Doubleday, trans. John Veitch, p. 47-48 and 55.

AFTER ALBERTA (I)
STILL (T)HERE BY ANNE MALENA

THERE WAS BANFF AND THE correspondence,
or the journey, through *Deuils cannibales
et mélancoliques* and *Pornographies*.[1] An
encounter entre les langues and a mutual
recognition of their failure to remain
separate, to reassure us of the possibility
of translation. You worried about the
ethics of transposing not only the book
but the author as well. I struggled with
the desire to transport both the author
and myself into the language we live in, by
choice or circumstance. We climbed the
mountain behind the residence and walked
downhill into town, talking, always talking,
scratching out a place for our conversation

to continue in the space of the in-
between, the inachevé, the unmeshed.
And we are still (t)here.

Many words later came Edmonton
and your opening with "the failure of
translation". I had traveled from the gift
of *Paper City* to *Touch to Affliction*, moved
by the desire to know, to understand.
But "in a Paper City write nothing
down" (*Paper City* 23)[2] and in the ruins
of the city "we are walking backwards
into our lives" (*Touch to Affliction* 9). In
between there was *Je Nathanaël* and the
"transformations that inhabit us" as well
as the act of self-translation. The surprise
for me, who had only read him in school
as part of the canon, was the influence of
André Gide and the realization that he
makes limpid sense. My resistance may
have been linked to having assimilated
a certain malaise I detected in my
teachers since he didn't fit easily into the
comfortable category of dead white great

male writers. He too dwelled in between genre, gender and social norms. He too searched for an ethics of that space for, as I discern now while rereading *Je Nathanaël*, isn't that the perfect locus within which to situate oneself in an attempt to formulate a moral philosophy of right and wrong? The choice to live and write neither here nor there is an ethical one but it fails, as it must, not being a final choice, to provide answers to the questions: "Is there an ethics of desire? An ethics of language? Where one begins does the other really end?" (*Je Nathanaël* 7). The failure of translation is linked to this since it is made up of mostly impossible choices that prevent it from remaining in the in-between and force it too quickly to step into the other, dangerously ignoring the obstacles in its way. The text is destroyed in the process and its afterlife depends on the ethics of the translator and the other as it is handed over in trust and safe keeping:

> *Fragments of an amphora which are to be glued together must match one another in the smallest details, although they need not be like one another. In the same way a translation, instead of resembling the meaning of the original, must lovingly and in detail incorporate the original's mode of signification, thus making both the original and the translation recognizable as fragments of a greater language, just as fragments are part of an amphora.* (Walter Benjamin, quoted in Derrida, 1988, p. 119)[3]

To read Benjamin in translation leads to confusion and erasure of swatches of his thought. What is that "amphora", which by definition is kept half buried in the earth? Did Derek Walcott read Benjamin in English when he wrote the passage below about history?

> *Break a vase, and the love that reassembles the fragments is stronger than that love which took its symmetry for granted when it was whole. The glue that fits the pieces is the sealing of its original shape.* (*The Antilles*, no page number)[4]

My own practice of reading led to the juxtaposition of these two texts long ago but I have never been secure in my interpretation of these echoes until you spoke to me and later evoked in a classroom of kabbalah, the light and the vessel. According to kabbalah the cosmos was first filled by a ubiquitous and omnipotent light, whose sole function was giving because such "is the essential nature of the Light: to expand in every direction, and to endlessly share of itself".[5] The vessel was created out of the light to be its instrument of giving but developed the desire to receive for itself alone and had to be violently destroyed, shattered in fact. Those remaining shards continued to reflect the light, offering the possibility of reconstituting the desire to receive as a desire to receive with the aim of giving and sharing. The amphora/vase has, therefore, to be the vessel of the kabbalah: the reciprocal love of and for the light is the only hope for translation to be carried safely across and for the history of an oppressed people to shine through the imposed darkness of European history:

> *The sigh of History rises over ruins, not over landscapes, and in the Antilles there are few ruins to sigh over, apart from the ruins of sugar estates and abandoned forts. […] A century looked at a landscape furious with vegetation in the wrong light and with the wrong eye. […] History can alter the eye and the moving hand to conform a view of itself; it can rename places for the nostalgia in an echo; it can temper the glare of tropical*

> *light to elegiac monotony in prose,*
> *the tone of judgement in Conrad,*
> *in the travel journals of Froude.*
> *[…] It [tristesse, the mood in Lévi-*
> *Strauss'* Tristes Tropiques*] relates to*
> *a misunderstanding of the light and*
> *the people on whom the light falls.*
> (Walcott)

The power of the metaphor resides in the inextricability it maintains between hope and death, destruction and possibility, shimmers of resistance and the obscurity of repression. The space of the in-between is traversed by the bright and dark lights of opposing sides that are no longer opposed. Translation struggles to escape, aspires to recover the original light but cannot help dragging along its path the tragic remnants of the destruction leading to its very necessity. Benjamin, Walcott and Nathanaël know this only too well.

Then came a new turn, *The Sorrow and*

the Fast of It, a translation that isn't one with . . .*s'arrête? Je* and *L'absence au lieu (Claude Cahun et le livre inouvert)* with its own translation already inscribed within it. And for me an almost insurmountable task to talk of the first two, because of knowledge, because of experience, because of sharing, because of life. All those reasons also make it possible as the books themselves show. And I, not a writer but a critic, "not so much want as want not" to comment (*The Sorrow and the Fast of It* 9). The walking book becomes a livre erreur of which I cannot speak. But the translated failure of language is supplemented with échouer, running aground, an arrival that leads nowhere, not a departure. This book leads to suicide, to the erasure of the self within the cities, all those that remain unnameable. So we meet again, this time in death and the remembrance of it. I long ago willed for myself that arrival to become a departure. The choice had

everything to do with giving although
I knew nothing of the kabbalah then.
And the erroneous book was returned
to me. The terrible responsibility of that
gift, the awesome clarity of my response,
the inextricable encounter of suicide
and survival, the lack of awareness of
the interdiction that ensued, the vague
awareness of a shift, un glissement.
But I notice that "A mark of singular
unimportance" becomes "Une marque
d'importance singulière" and "is it
possible to love without leaving?" turns
into "est-il possible d'aimer sans se
mouvoir [s'émouvoir?]?" (*The Sorrow* 6
and 11; … *s'arrête? Je* 14 and 17). I also
notice that my keyboard must be French
in order to write this English text while
switching back and forth. It even learns to
do it on its own, a tiny victory. So perhaps
the interdiction was unnecessary, perhaps
the failure of language marks all of us
in these un/important ways, keeps us
alive, leaving us moved and in perpetual

movement.

So the space for exchange and dialogue is transformed somewhat with no resolution in sight since none is desired. The correspondence is amplified, swollen with various kinds of writing, with grief, history, humour often, silences, readings, missed calls, all the sadness of the past and the present, the questions of leaving, healing, despairing, staying. I learn and think about the "heart's sudden seizure. The compression of centuries into one solid moment of bereavement" (*The Sorrow* 42) and I unlearn anew, and this time along with my students, the certainties of genre, gender, identity, the body, history, language and more. I come and fetch you at the arrivals' gate and a week later I bring you back to the departure level. In between the space is filled with thoughts and talks and dialogue and mostly indigestible food and many rich moments, all of it public yet always private. A problem of performance: can we ever get away from the simulacra? They read you, do they really? They receive you, they continue to do so. They perceive you, in so many ways. They accept to be disturbed, disrupted, arrested or they don't. It matters, it matters so much. No one asks why ALÉA? Why don't I when day after day I wonder about why un coup de dés jamais n'abolira le hasard? A few months earlier I wrote somewhere else and I now translate that le hasard can pounce on us at every turn, that through encounters, decisions, choices, we manage to stay more or less open to chance, to unexplainable, undesired, even undesirable events, that no matter how many times we throw the dice, chance will never be overcome, understood, explained. The thought had come from somewhere else and unexpectedly resurfaces here, comes close but ALÉA isn't that either. Students write about their bodies in Edmonton, some understand the need, discover something hidden, wander in wonder, most don't bother, don't see it, maybe don't let themselves feel it, maybe they will later. In the city "there is one poem and the poets keep writing it" and with that you belong, in spite of yourself, to this, which "is not an accommodation, this is the ironic republic that is poetry" (Walcott). I think of Le Corbusier, a native son from where I escaped, and of how he might have felt in cities, how he needed to resolve the unease, to abolish chance, to ensure no one escaped, anywhere, to make us all participate. But you want slippage and ALÉA is built upon the dismantling of architecture, its dis/solution into fluidity. I remember being vaguely aware of a shift, which I keep on resisting. I first wrote: Algiers' rooftops provide another space for the in-between, the inachevé, the unmeshed, this time named the paradoxical, the privileged space between public and private, the possibility to

shield oneself from the colonial gaze
and throw it back. Something's wrong. I
return to ALÉA and stare at "a place that
is not intermediary, but [...] a space of
reiterative ending. It is neither between,
nor outside, but is accomplished in defeat,
in dismemberment, in infinite finitude".
Ironically you have moved on, not I. The
intermediary has been defining me, has
guided my hands to write about the in-
between and the colonial gaze, nudges me
to wonder sadly, reading *The Translator*
by Leila Aboulela, whether those rooftops
remain or whether, like their Egyptian
counterparts, they are being built upon to
house more people since "no one sleeps
outside anymore" (146)[6]. But, of course,
what matters, whether they still exist or
not, is that they figure the space where the
I and writing keep undoing themselves.
For now all I can do is accept the
difference within the space that I continue
to think we share, my desire, my inability
to enter infinite finitude.

Light again plays a role here for the rooftop metaphorical dweller, offering both illumination and the glare of opacity, understanding and occlusion. Like Edouard Glissant, claiming the right to opacity, the rooftop writer rejects transparency. There is no need for it anyway once its impossibility is understood, once the space where both arrest and unrest happen is accepted but can it ever be? Accepted? I know it can't, that it has to remain suspended between illusion and void that it is as ephemeral as the writing that depends on it. But I again resist the notion of suicide, its suggestion of finality in spite of the beauty, is that the word?, that can be found in it. My own need to arrest, to seek transitory relief from constant unrest generates my desire to remain there, to give in however briefly to contemplation, to let a glimmer of hope filter through. Beauty may well be, after all, in the eye of

the beholder. Seeing it in the writing and
not seeing it in the roof or cliff jumper
keeps me alive. Almost reluctantly I move
from the rooftop back to the book, to
Absence Where As, which I haven't read,
having opened instead and wandered into
*L'absence au lieu (Claude Cahun et le livre
inouvert)*.

Lastly, although there is no final
ending, came discussions and disguised
expectations, of audience, of venue,
of translation practice and of so much
more. All that remained to do was to let
them happen, invite them to take place
as it were in a difficult space, mixed
with exhaustion, friendships, questions,
reflections. The dédoublement du
personnage was doubled and dubbed
through photography more than
language, for once. A pleasant, albeit
slightly disturbing, surprise that would
surface later when here and there were
briefly wrenched apart before settling

back down in their inextricability. That evening translation exploded, dropping a multitude of shards on all of us. I saw a few people pick them up and contemplate them closely, perhaps looking for their own image in the reflecting light. Some found something and bought books. Others lingered, bewildered. In that space I remembered your affirmation: "je maintiens ici, en ce lieu où je suis, en ce livre où je fuis, le droit au désordre" (*L'absence au lieu* 24). Lines will lose their definition in spite of being drawn, translation will not be in spite of being. I asked why does translation have to end since it can be the undoing of stasis, the expression of unendings. I like the answer, the risk of confining oneself, de se contenter, to the artifice of an exercise. No, if language defines you, you can also define it as you wrote in the first person and I translate in the second. Claude Cahun, who bore almost the same name as the forebear born on the rooftops,

is your first and second person and an
exercise she or he is not. The resemblance
isn't superficial but embodied in both of
you, or should I say the four of you or
none of you, past and present.

The photograph interpellates[7] you and
rejects you, threatens to engulf you
into madness. What happens within
the trajectory of the gaze is almost
unbelievable since this ineffable and
unbearable space fills up with echoes of
history, memory, rejected lineage de part
et d'autre, a correspondence that annuls
the I in its absorption into the other I.
As a result you read and reread yourself,
hanging on to previous expressions of
the I, however problematized and self-
destructive they have been. The violence
of the encounter seems to ease somewhat
but soon returns you to the city. At that
point in *L'absence au lieu*, I wonder where
does that put me? The question seems
out of place, yet I know why it is posed;

I know what's coming and I want to stop reading, so what am I afraid of? Of losing my own I? Why would that be? I vaguely remember once being confronted with an old fashioned silhouette profile and being told that it looked like me. Both the picture and the suggestion still haunt me. So we are that fragile but I know that and cities are difficult to negotiate but I know that also. Is it I resisting the text or the text resisting me? Reading on then. Many cities because of the possibility for numerous encounters and this, brought up in a classroom, the negation of the capital city because, quite simply, it affects or involves the loss of, the head or life. A dictionary definition that for once borders on nonsense. Cahun denies the capital encounter by saying that she or he lived through it without seeing it if naming it so didn't sufficiently indicate that it cannot be survived. Photographs mean fixity, which needs to be rejected again and again. Yet, like translation, I think

that is also an illusion and that returning
to it over and over again forces the fixity
to surrender. That is both frightening and
a relief.

I'll end where I started. With the
untranslatable "Je n'en reviens pas"
(*L'absence au lieu* 81), full of amazement
at the impossibility of returning, which I
often recall in my "Je te reviens", whether
I do come back or not. My absences are
brief as are yours. The absence of place
inhabits us and yet, we create a lieu
where we are, a surrogate, a space instead
of another, somewhere from where it
remains possible to escape. The we is
presumptuous, transitory, undone as soon
as it is offered, always, with anyone. So
there you are and here I am. And yet, at
Alberta, out of Alberta, we are still (t)here.

1. Catherine Mavrikakis, *Deuils cannibales et mélancoliques*. Laval : Éditions Trois, 2000. Translated as *A Cannibal and Melancholy Mourning*. Toronto: Coach House Books, 2004. Claudine Potvin, *Pornographies*. Québec: L'Instant même, 2002.

2. Also the disappeared title for a seminar on the Capital City.

3. Jacques Derrida, *The Ear of the Other*. Christie McDonald, ed. Peggy Kamuf, trans. Lincoln and London: Nebraska UP, 1988.

4. Derek Walcott, *The Antilles: Fragments of Epic Memory, The Nobel Lecture*. New York: Farrar, Strauss and Giroux, 1992.

5. http://www.kabbalah.com/k/index.php/p=life/religion. Use of this reference doesn't imply that I subscribe to its message of faith.

6. Leila Aboulela, *The Translator*. Oxford: Heinemann, 1999.

7. This word, used widely in Film Studies, since it was borrowed from the French, as were many theories in the field in the Sixties, continues to repel spellcheck, so its presence is essential here.

AFTER ALBERTA (II)
WHAT ARCHITECTURES OF
URGENCY DO YOU RAISE?
AND THEN RAZE? WITH
CHRISTINE STEWART

SOME QUESTIONS FOR NATHANAËL

I'm thinking about you reading and rereading, always returning (and returning) to Benjamin's "Theses on the Philosophy of History."

This morning I have these questions:

Do you write in a "state of emergency"? Do you write to bring about "a real state of emergency" (as Benjamin puts it)? Even as I use these words I feel their constraints in English, their histories, the way they contain, simplify (gag) what is urgent, what really matters (what might materialize here). I hear the echoes of George Bush after 911, New Orleans, the assaults on Islamic women, the ideologies of hysteria that work towards a politics of fear, of manipulation, neglect and control. And this is NOT what you do. In French: a state of urgency, "état d'urgence." For me this is better—less gagging. And so then this question, how do you read Benjamin's theses—in French or English? […] How do the perimeters of these words change in French? What was it to be Nabokov and speak eight or nine languages? This is where morality and its limits of brain and bone and origin are cruel. […] For you, where do class and its bodies meet?

Is it naïve to say that this awareness, this state of urgency will change how we do things in the future? If it is, then what does this presentation, embodiment of urgency do? Can we even ask such a question? What does it mean to do? Okay, what about this? *What architectures of urgency do you raise? And then raze?*

A […] question: does your mother read you?

Your "I" is interesting to me having being brought up (albeit peripherally) on a poetics that decries the use of the subject (the I). For you, it seems as if this is the critical point at which all ruination and delineations must take place.

[…]

What and where does your text shed? And I suppose I could also ask what or where does your text hut?

In Jean Luc Nancy's *L'Intrus* he writes (and I am reading this in translation. (Phillip M. Adamek) I can't find the page number because Project Muse has just bumped me off and I can't find the other copy. I'll keep looking): "[T]he subject is its exteriority and its excessiveness: its infinite exposition." Does this explain somewhat why you inhabit, or in fact, do not inhabit (do you haunt?) a subject position? Are you writing/dusting/tasting the exteriors of the subject? This is an impossible question, full of holes and so I will leave it as such. How do you understand the idea of the posthuman? Or do you?

TO CHRISTINE, UNFOLDING (YOUR QUESTIONS)

Immediately (*maintenant*), there is this from Nancy, which I turn to on the heels of your manifold question / exposition: "La vérité du sujet est son extériorité et son excessivité: son exposition infinie." But there is more: "L'intrus m'expose excessivement. Il m'extrude, il m'exporte, il m'exproprie." These last two lines become residual only because they are absent from this part of your question (a departure?), and possibly

from the inaccessible Project Muse article
by Adamek (which and whom I have
not read). These lines *in excess* – [de
trop] – "outside" of the text are at least as
significant as those you quote. Its "infinite
exposition" is recuperated, or else abated
or held back by the turn to the excessive,
that the infinite could do violence in this
way, by over-exposing. And this excess
is gathered into the following terms:
"extrudes, exports, expropriates". The life
of the body withheld, postponed, *dans
l'attente (l'attentat).* Nancy is waiting for
a new heart (*cardiacus*), for a carcinogen,
that will enable the settlement of the
foreign organ into the body, which holds
a place, in absence (and in abeyance),
for a thing that is already expired and
anticipating its own expiration. There
is the violence of excavation and the
violence of implantation, each of which
open endlessly onto endless possible
deaths. (To domesticate the new heart
there is need also to poison the body

that houses it. Might this be the elusive subject's ill-fitted dwelling?) It might be here, precisely, that the text sheds, that it comes apart in those raised / razed architectures, of excess and inadequacy (the hard parts gone soft?), on the (crumbling?) edge of your festering lake – a literal (if not literary) littoral. There is a moment in John Zorn's *Bar Kokhba* where the violin screams. I think of this when reading *À l'écoute*, reading this into your question, also, of Benjamin's *état d'urgence* and Arvo Pärt's *Fratres*, as though brotherhood or fraternity could only be articulated discordantly (invective, admonition, mercenary). Between what I hear and what I listen to, the ways in which I am attentive, the battle fields soak up their share(s) of blood. (Here, Le Corbusier intrudes with his seamless and seemingly unthinking passage from the battle field to the wheat field as though the caterpillars in question did not carry with them Goya's mangled,

maddened bodies – abodes?). George
Steiner (*Real Presences*) wants the text as
homeland – "In dispersion", he writes,
"the text is homeland". Is this another
form of bloodletting? "All history," he
annouces a few pages later, "is 'housed'
in the grammar of the past tense." We
are far now from Benjamin's abiding
now, [*nunc stans*] and Steiner's proofs
are made in apposition: if grammar
(totalism) is a form of lodging (enclosure
and encapsulation), then it can only be
grappled with as ruin, as discontinuous,
as a welcome degradation of its own
murderous constructions (think of Speer
and Hitler's plans for a crumbling empire;
LE PLAN, which Le Corbusier eerily
defines years earlier as LE DICTATEUR
– caps his.). The lines (of blood) running
between family, nation and state are
incontrovertible, and to still dream
such a dream (today – aujourd'hui, per
Bachmann) is to invigorate (the body's
– willed?) devastation. (With […], we

have an understanding: she reads me as she wishes to (very closely, but from a distance, since […]) and resists asking (me) the sorts of questions the text might be asking (of) her.) Regarding the boots, I might be inclined to go bare foot. Pronominally, I think that it is not (not) possible to (not) say I (je). The displacement of guilt onto the fictional outside does not avenge anyone or anything, and simply displaces the question of place away from the body (and guilt away from its own problematic). If we cannot say I then perhaps we give (ourselves) permission to relinquish accountability. I have come to understand that English is uncomfortable with self-referentiality; if it is not possible (recourse to a passive construction) to look directly at one another, ragefully, fearfully, affectionately, desirously, then we cannot look either at ruination, nor dwell there as perhaps we must. It is the question I understand Claude Cahun to

be posing, when from the past present she
looks at me, mimics me, abolishes me from
the very place where I might be settling
into the throes of disengaged complacency.
This ties back, I think, to the state of
emergency, and Nancy, this especially:
"Cette présence est donc toujours dans
le renvoi et la rencontre. Elle se renvoie à
soi, elle se rencontre ou, mieux, elle se fait
contre soi, à son encontre et tout contre.
Elle est co-présence ou encore 'présence en
présence,' si l'on peut dire."[1]

discutere

April 7, 2008

Yes, the [...] Fens. [...] The people of the
Fens near Norfolk lived in stilt houses and
travelled by boat. [...] ask my 102 year old
grandmother and she will tell you that Fen
people were [...]. I have some questions

and I thought I should [...]. Could be that our "interview" won't work as you need it to. If so, time is getting short for you to sort out a different configuration. I listened to part of the tape. It's nice but [...] I'm glad you liked (or something) *L'Intrus*. Nancy is excruciating ([...]).

C.

April 7, 2008

[...] kept thinking of a text we would [...], composed possibly of letters [...], that might be [...] and literally upon sitting before the screen, whatever was beginning to [...] in the dishwater vanished and I could only [...] I will nonetheless look at these questions and respond to them if only to prove [...]

Here is something: the Latin, *discutere*, means "to dash to pieces" – here we

are with those chips or shards (my
substitution) of Benjamin's [...] Might
our "interview" turn to letters, in pieces?
We could certainly continue like this,
[...], and to hell with [...] which makes
me think immediately for some reason
of Hervé Guibert's cancerous image in
the form of a stolen [...] of a young boy
drained of the image after months of
exposure to the air and his own [...],
where he taped it against his skin for days
until he couldn't [...], only to find the
image had transferred onto his skin, and
the paper was [...] again – is this love?).

N.

April 7, [...]

[...] Email is [...]. Someone, somewhere
called [...] Larkin's [...] *Walking* a romp
and I'd say [...] closer to my reading so
far – [dégringolade]. I like the idea of

discutere: dashing […] letters to pieces. And you can decline or dash any question ([…] proximities you choose), as it pleases you, for it should please you. […] I cannot keep my subject in it's objective […] an easy shard. […] And at some time, for some time I imagined (and believed) that that was all it was. But I'm not so sure any more. […]

C.

April 8, 2008

[…] though "sense" and "limit" were among the last terms caught in the net of feigned systematization, […] Now, though, maintenant, oh and this reminds me: (Nancy, again, re. Husserl's "présent vivant"): "Ce présent est le maintenant d'un sujet qui donne, en première ou en dernière instance, sa présence au présent, ou son présent à la présence." (*À l'écoute*)

[…] I lugged home with me a copy of
[…] *La Ville Radieuse*, odious, curious
object, dedicated to, […] L'AUTORITÉ.

[…]

[…] it - he - may not be a person at all
but pure fabrication. Still, […] exists in
the world, and therefore in my exhausting
dreams of holocausts all mixed up with
desire, and it would appear our […]
together has been indefinitely postponed.
A dead dream? Perhaps not, if […], not
dead but *moriendo* – "ce n'est pas en
finissant, c'est en infinissant".

Nathanaël

April 8

[…] of what I said was true. That […] a
fever. […] I want to speak of […]. That
when I wrote fucking […] neither […]

or figuratively. That […] could be mine. That you claim […] yours and so […] yours in a dream […] dead and not […] but postponing. That as such […] are dead, postponed […] nothing so that they […] at all […] the first place or […] last […]

"if you consider him in his right to existence in itself, this right is immediately to the same degree a right not to be, since such is the right of a being that does not have its capacity to be in itself (and that is, therefore, a capacity not to be)."

(Suhrawardi in Agamben's *Potentialities*)

[…].

April [8], 2008

When did […] become […]? […] […], with Nancy, again – "C'est un présent en

vague sur un flot, non en point sur une
ligne, c'est un temps qui s'ouvre, qui se
creuse et qui s'élargit ou se ramifie, qui
enveloppe et qui sépare, qui met ou qui se
met en boucle, qui s'étire ou se contracte,
etc." (*À l'écoute*).

Bachmann had something to say about
suicide – your "capacity not to be" (is [...]
can capacity be willed?) – in the present,
([...], [...] maintenant) – and on my way
to the bookshelf and back, I realised I had
(temporarily, temporally) subsituted now
[...] for today, her word. [...] "Actually,
anything written about Today should
be destroyed immediately, just like all
real letters are crumpled or torn up,
unfinished and unmailed, all because they
were written but cannot arrive, Today."
[...] But more to the point, [...], on
suicide: "In fact, 'today' is a word which
only suicides ought to be able to use; it
has no meaning for other people." And
so on until [t]oday's teology [...] its "final

hour". Irrevocable. Not Gabriel's capacity to not be, or else be. [...] (When do we stop?)

N.

[...], 2008

But I also want to say [...] everything I have [...] is true. [...] I'm [...]. What else [...] When I [said] fucking I heard [...] moves [...] how [...] body [...] frightening [...] and [gorgeous] This I do [...] understand. When I said text [...] not literature [...] not text this was absurdity and [...] it was [...] true nor [...] It has no need [...] they must [...] dead letters spoken [...] perhaps the speaking [...] out loud [...] changes [...] I don't know [...] like boy [...] the word man [...]–and woman. [...]. And email [...].its intimacy [...] no body, [...] face, [...] mouth, no laughter. And Bartleby did commit suicide [...] his will to not [...].

"Benjamin discerns the inner correspondence between copying and the eternal return when he compares Nietzsche's concept to die Strafe des Nachsitzens, that is, the punishment assigned by the teacher to negligent schoolchildren that consists in copying out the same text countless times ("The eternal return is copying projected onto the cosmos. Humanity must copy out its texts in innumerable repetitions.") The infinite repetition of what was abandons all potential not to be. The will to power is, in truth, the will to will, an eternally repeated action; only as such is it potentialized. This is why the scrivner must stop copying, why he must give up his work." (*Potentialities* 268)

The will to will, the eternally repeated [...]. I think we should read [Arendt].

C.

I want for you to have the last word. The last word of our [dead] letters?

N.

[…]

C.

1. "This presence is thus always within return and encounter. It *returns* (refers) to *itself*, it *encounters* itself or, better, occurs against itself, both in opposition to and next to itself. It is co-presence, or again, "presence in presence," if one can say that." (Trans. Charlotte Mandell).

ACKNOWLEDGEMENTS

The texts collected in this book were delivered at the University of Alberta in the context of the 2006 edition of the Annual Translation Conference and of a subsequent Distinguished Visitorship in 2008 (March 30 – April 4), both hosted by the Department of Modern Languages and Cultural Studies.

With one exception:
The CORRESPONDANCES text.
It has no place.

WANT : L'INTRADUISIBLE, the keynote lecture delivered at the translation conference, was also delivered at Poets House (NYC), in the context of its Conversations on Poetics series (2006). A version of this talk was published in Drunken Boat 9.

CORRESPONDANCES was commissioned for an issue of *Spirale Magazine* for inclusion in its dossier, Write Here, Write Now. Les écritures anglo-montréalaises (No 210, Sept/Oct 2006). Fragments of it subsist here in this book, with some alteration.

AFTER ALBERTA (I) & (II) transpired from synchronous and deferred correspondences with Anne Malena and Christine Stewart.

FRONTISPIECE and acknowledgements photo by Sina Queyras (c. 2008).

COROLLARY ACCOLADES to Lynn Penrod, Yukari Fukuchi Meldrum, Marianne Henn, Jay MillAr.

COLOPHON

Manufactured by BookThug in an edition of 500 copies in the fall of 2008. Distributed in Canada by the Literary Press Group. Distributed in the US by Small Press Distribution. Shop on-line at
WWW.BOOKTHUG.COM

Designed by Jay MillAr.